AF379567

All Great Things
Things

I Learned on the Farm

Curtis A. Johnson

Curtis A. Johnson

2

Copyright © 2023
All Rights Reserved

Dedication

I would like to dedicate my book to my grandchildren. This would include Everette, Mackenzie, Madilyn (deceased), Briella, and Natalie. They are my legacy, and hopefully, the values I have developed will be embraced by them as they inherit their piece of our great planet. I very much believe in the "pass it on" concept of doing good things as you journey through life. I hope they will share in the feelings that I have expressed in this book.

Table of Contents

About the Author

The author, a gentleman raised on a small farm in southern Wisconsin, cultivated an insatiable curiosity from an early age. Balancing his religious upbringing with a strong affinity for scientific understanding, he dedicated his life to unraveling the mysteries of existence. Through his profound journey, he discovered the meaning of life, the integration of spiritual values, and the truth about what happens after death. This book is the culmination of his quest, offering his enlightening answers to these fundamental questions.

Preface

This writing will be my first attempt at humor and sharing the many life lessons I have learned. Growing up on a farm, I found that these occurrences and experiences establish a basic theme with life and often provide a person with valuable learnings. Learnings that you will use repeatedly throughout life. Telling the whole story that goes with each incident offers humor and some lessons.

Chapter 1: My Start

My beginnings go back to a small farm in Southern Wisconsin. The farm was near a small town called Hebron. While multiple towns have the same name, there is also Hebron in Illinois. It is more crowded and much better known because whenever I would mention that name, people would denote Illinois as my home state until I would correct them.

My parents were raised on farms during childhood and spent their entire lives in a rural/agricultural setting. The early parts of my story are not entirely from my memories; instead, they come from tales and stories I was told about those early years.

It all started on an arid and scorching September day when I decided it was time for my appearance in life. The day was 3rd September 1953. My mother was a very gentle and quiet lady in all mannerisms, except when some drama would suddenly enter her life. I am told that the day I was born was going along as any other day, and suddenly, with my kicks and movements, it became clear the time was now. My father had to be called in from working on the fall harvest, so when he arrived back at our house, my parents jumped into the old Ford and began their hasty trip to the hospital in Fort Atkinson.

My dad told stories that while my mother never swore or had a bad word for anyone, she made an exception that day. While she seldom used them, she knew a lot of bad words. My dad spoke of people a great distance down the hall from the delivery room but was still well within hearing range of the screams and yelling mixed with some spicy cursing. Despite not generally mouthing a cuss word, my mother knew them all.

And then suddenly, there I was, a new member of the 'baby boomers' generation. From the somewhat vague record in those times, I was pretty much standard regarding all birth statistics. I still have a copy of the hospital bill, which all fit on a small piece of paper and totaled about $60.00. In today's world, that would not cover more than two aspirins.

Our home was a modest farmhouse. It was one bedroom with one small bath and an attic or second floor that could be made livable. It was 1953, and I suspect the house was built just around the time of the great depression, so it was functional and very frugal. I mentioned the upstairs, which would later become two bedrooms, and when you stood up, you either stayed in the middle of the room or banged your head on the angled ceiling, which was the roof line with some plaster added.

There was no heat and no cooling for most of our time there. Before our use of this upstairs, we all shared the one bedroom that was on the first floor. It was tiny and would fit a full-sized bed and one small crib.

It would be 15 months later that my sister came along, and we all still shared that one bedroom for many years. Now this is where one of my more profound questions in life comes from. Was my sister conceived while I watched? It is a rather curious thought; it could even be the source of some emotional concerns. As I think more about this, it explains why only one sister exists. My psychiatrist may suggest this was my very first repressed memory. But as the owl profoundly stated as he was licking the tootsie roll pop (to determine the number of licks it took to get to the chewy center), "The world may never know." And, I have no lessons learned here other than to ponder this great mystery of how many licks it takes to get to the center of a tootsie pop.

In addition to the house, we had a barn, a granary, a tool and farm machinery shed, and a chicken house. At that time, living in southern Wisconsin, it was a typical farm and building and was meant to be run and managed by one family with occasional help from a neighbor.

The dining room was the largest of the rooms in the house, and in retrospect, I think it was related to the fact that during this time, you shared work with other neighbors, and when they were working or helping on your farm, you fed them.

Of course, you always put out the best dishware and silverware whenever you served a guest a meal. It provided a brief respite from the heat and toil of the day and was a primary form of socialization in those times. You got together, enjoyed a large meal, and discussed everything from a neighbor three miles away to a review of their family tree. I recall these as good times and one that, if not for socialization, at least was a meal that was lavish and excessive. This was a time when you would impress your neighbors.

There was never a time when you went away hungry from one of these meals. It is interesting to think about this time from a historical perspective. There were many small farms, and often due to the financial lack of resources, a single farmer could not afford the equipment needed to grow and harvest crops or raise a herd or flock of some animal.

This caused people to be cooperative and to share work, equipment, and other resources they may have. People got along very well and could work closely together, share equipment, and prosper by working together. You always knew all your neighbors, and there was never a time when you passed by them that you did not give a small wave or nod of the head to say 'Hi.'

There was no personal gain by anyone unless there was group gain. This is a lesson that today's very evolved and developed society could recall and benefit from. We all very much depended upon the support and work of one another and would only succeed if everyone simultaneously succeeded. In our present times, not only is the group or community effort gone, but we have come to feel that our self-gain is acceptable at another person's loss. I would say that presently, we strive to dominate others, and if it comes at another's expense, this is okay. Our society could benefit greatly if we could return to these previous times and values.

Curtis A. Johnson

Chapter 2: The Young Years

The first notable event in my life, which my parents liked to tell me about, was also the one that ended with my very first spanking. Yes, in those good old days, you did get spankings.

And, yes, they were not pleasant, but they were rare, and when you got one, you knew you did wrong, very wrong. I do believe in the saying, "Spare the rod and spoil the child." And somewhat, at times to my dismay, my parents believed in that same old saying.

While I do not believe in harsh punishment nor anything that would even remotely cause bodily harm, part of understanding the difference between good and bad in life is knowing there are consequences when you do something terrible.

As it was told to me, my sister had arrived into the world and was just coming home for her first time.

I was already walking and had already developed an extraordinary sense of curiosity or a need to know everything. So, with my sister wrapped in blankets and set upon a table, that curiosity took over and guided me to seek out and see what this strange new thing was, which was in a blanket and was moving and making noise all by itself. I am sure this was a fascinating and completely curious moment since I had not, prior to that time, seen, heard, or experienced another tiny human being. Until then, I was an only child, and given our "stay at home" propensity, I had not seen nor experienced other babies.

I was very surprised by this miniature little person making noise and equally as surprised when I grabbed these blankets and pulled them to see what this new wonder was. In an almost instant, the second great surprise I received was a swat on my behind. A substantial hand it was.

As I stated previously, I do not remember this event, maybe more repressed memories, but I am told that I was not a happy camper for the next several minutes. My takeaway from this is that fear is a great motivator. While I was in a learning mode at the time, the fear of that big hand instantly became a strong motivator not to do things that may be improper. This is especially true when it comes to a young man who does not like a sore behind. Now I know modern society teaches us that a spanking is harmful, and you are supposed to work with your child to reason and build understanding, but let me tell you, a smack on the behind creates a pretty fast understanding that there are things you should not do and that you do things you are told to do when you are told to do them.

You just plain don't forget these lessons for the rest of your life.

The other fact about this new little person in the blankets is that I now have a partner in crime. You know, things are always better when there is someone else to share your experiences with.

And being the older brother, I needed to be the brains of these operations. I do recall a few moments from this time, and for those which I forgot, I was told some subsequently good stories based upon what I did and what I let my sister to do. Like any good leader, you seek to find the boundaries of your universe.

In being a leader, you must be brave, take risks, face dangers, and reach out to new challenges and new lands. Of course, the first thing this means is that you find a way out of your crib. Now, recalling the fear element, apparently, I did find my way out of my crib and was equally as clever at getting back in before being discovered.

One of my memories during this time was that there was this much larger thing called a house, and there was much to explore in this house. Things were all new to me and all so large and a bit scary. I am pretty sure the reason I remained safe during this time was that my mother was a good housewife and therefore spent much of her time in the house and watching over us.

She even timed our naps to coincide with any outside choirs she needed to do and felt that while we were asleep, we were safe if she was doing other things. Very recently in life, I had the opportunity to view a video of my then 15-month-old Grandson, Everette.

It was very interesting; he had just discovered the full body mechanics of flipping a leg over the edge of his crib, using that weight and momentum to carry his other leg then over and, lastly next, his full body over the railing of his crib. He would then drop to the floor, one arm holding onto the crib rail to slow his descent. And the entire time is laughing his best and biggest laugh of all time. Yes, he had escaped the dreaded jail crib and was now free to return to being awake and avoiding his nap. His parents, while amazed and somewhat shocked, could only join in his laughter as he ran off to continue his play elsewhere.

Now, back to me, this must have been the same euphoria that I felt when I escaped from behind the bars of my crib.

As my sister and I grew older, one of the most exciting things to do was to go spying. You know, if you go through all the work to escape the crib prison, there must be something you are seeking to do or see beyond just the thrill of the escape.

My sister/accomplice and I would sneak out of our crib and slowly, ever so slowly, crawl about the house, using the furniture for cover. We would ultimately come to a location where we could watch our parents and whatever they were doing without being seen.

As I have grown older, I suspect they may have known we were there, but perhaps, they just joined in the game and allowed us to feel we were undetected and pretend they did not know they were being watched. We would start by watching my mother. She would always read the daily newspaper and catch up on who died. Yes, that was always the first section she read.

She would comment to my dad about someone whom I never knew and how young they were to die. She would next review this person's entire line of relatives and friends and their status of alive or dead. My father would grumble something but never really seemed very interested. As she continued to read the paper, she would get sleepy, and suddenly and ever so slowly, the paper would simply crumple into her lap.

For us kids, this was as exciting as it could be. We were doing something we knew we should not be doing; we were hiding and getting away with it. Best of all, we were watching our mom try to read the paper through closed eyelids.

Slowly the paper would sink, then suddenly, just as if the earth shook, she would wake up with a start, the paper would shoot back up into reading position, and she would begin anew the attempt to read the paper.

This would go on for maybe an hour before she would finally cave in, go brush her teeth and head toward bed. This was always my sister's and mine que to sneak back quickly and get back into bed and pretend to be sleeping. You know, good spies never get caught and live to return for more espionage and spy work at a later time.

As I mentioned above, my dad was different from my mom, but he was also an interesting study during our espionage and surveillance moments. He was generally not a smoker but did enjoy a pipe full of tobacco each night.

Being a responsible parent, he would take his pipe in the bathroom with him and smoke in there with the door closed. The more curious thing was that this was his prime and only bathroom visit for the day.

It was a toxic combination of smells of feces and smoke. And it was always a 35-minute or longer activity. Even more curious for us spies was the fact that there was only one chair located in the bathroom, and it had a large hole in the center.

You would think that would be most uncomfortable. Now, at our young age, we had no knowledge of such a chair and what its purpose could possibly be. And from our limited observations, when you sit on this chair, you sit there with your pants down. We supposed this was for some reason, as well as convenience, if something special were going to happen.

Going back to his pipe, another curious thing is that it did not stay lit very well, and therefore, my dad, while in the bathroom for 30 to 40 minutes each evening, would need to relight the pipe frequently. Recall my earlier note that our house was small.

Well, trust me, the rest of the family learned that for those 35 minutes plus an added 15 minutes afterward, that bathroom was off-limits. It was uninhabitable. It does not take a lot of imagination but try to conjure up the aroma of cheap tobacco and an outhouse, all delicately mixed and left to hang in the air. Plus, having heat provided by an old wood furnace, there was almost no return air, just really a lot of hot air from the heat register.

Those two things may have been the very reason why the wallpaper kept peeling in that room. I do recall times that other family members had to make a trip to the great bathroom under the stars or beside a tree, as the one inside the house was uninhabitable at times. This was especially true when mother nature was not only calling, but she was screaming. Other than an occasional bat or mosquito, there was really nothing much to worry about.

My takeaway lesson here was when the old man was in the bathroom, it was no longer a community room. It was all his for as long as he wanted.

Eventually, I did learn what the hole in that great white chair in the bathroom was for. And that is one important lesson to learn.

Chapter 3: A Young Person's Lesson Some Things Can Hurt You

I now jump ahead a couple of years as my sister and I enter yet another brave new place in our world. It was called Outdoors.

As I look back, what we discovered happens to all animals on our planet. Once they can function independently, their mother will push them away and shun them to begin life on their own. In birds, they literally push them from the nest.

With humans, it takes a longer time, and it occurs in steps or phases. But when compared to the animal world, it basically is the same. Your parents start by telling you that you need to play outdoors or be outside, as did our parents. We found lots of things to do and, not so surprisingly, many things you could do to get hurt. One of the most painful moments in my life came when I found that you can take clay which is heavy, and make it into a ball. As it dries, it becomes almost like a rock and, in this case, a round ball.

After maybe a half day of drying, it is dried out and very strong.

One day, I made three clay dirt balls, each about 2 inches in diameter, and left them to harden in the sun. Later, I found they were very hard and not able to be broken. My small hands had crafted them, and while not knowingly potent, they could be used to throw and hit things. The first one I had launched at a tree, and with a very hard smack, it had exploded into tiny fragments of dirt and dust. But this did occur with a seemingly very hard impact on the tree before it broke. I decided to launch number 2 at one of our bath towels which was hanging on the clothesline.

Very much to my surprise, it hit the towel, the towel wrapped around it stopped its flight immediately and completely, and the ball dropped gently to the ground. It could be used again and again with no apparent damage. Over and over, I threw this clay bomb, each time trying to add new force and speed, a spin or a curve, and each time it flew into the towel, only to be enveloped and dropped to the ground harmlessly after encountering the towel.

This was the beginning of modern science and physics; I had discovered the throw the ball into a towel phenomenon. I had to share this with my sister. Remember, I was the leader of this pack. Every great inventor shares their inventions with society, and society, for me, was my sister. So, I talked her into coming over to the clothesline, explained just how to throw this tiny hard clay ball, and watched the bath towel literally catch it and drop it to the ground. She understood.

She took the ball as I stood at a right angle her; she wound up raising her arm full length and mustered up every last ounce of force she could, even taking a moment to focus on the towel and then let drive with her very essence and bang, I took that little ball right on the side of the mouth. Never in history had such a wild pitch been thrown.

That day I discovered two very important things in life. Neither of these lessons deals with physics, as you might suspect. The first learning is that girls only sometimes throw a ball straight. Second, despite the blood running from the side of my mouth, I learned that even if they were the cause of the injury, girls might still cry about it while not being hurt.

Yes, I am bleeding, my mouth is hurt, my clay ball lays on the ground, and my head hurts beyond compare, and my sister runs off crying to my mother because I had scared her. I guess science will have to wait for my other findings for now. I must listen to my mother scolding me while I endure the recently acquired pain and bloodshed.

Chapter 4: The Hunter

Growing up on the farm provides many opportunities to do many things.

One of my favorite pastimes was hunting. By the age of 11 I was already a pretty fair hunter, and I especially loved my BB gun. I had developed almost a sixth sense of where I was shooting and was a very fair marksman. I would easily take a 35-yard shot and pop a hole near the center in a bean can or something of similar size.

The problem was, a bean can become old hash quickly and I was looking for sincerer targets, you know, things that would break. And this was not good news for windows, bottles, and other breakable items around the farm.

Of course, windows do have a purpose, they keep weather outside. And when broken, not so much so. So, as I practiced more and more, I did have to buy a few replacement windowpanes.

Next came the white insulators on the electric fence, and, you guessed it, I had to buy and replace some to those. I finally learned that apples and knots in trees also make great targets and hitting those will not result in a financial cost. As a sense shooter, meaning shooting but without use of the sites for aiming, I did become very accurate. I do confess that there are probably many hundreds if not many thousands of spent BBs still laying in the dirt about the old farm.

Over time, I did progress to bigger and better weapons, my second gun being a .22 caliber rifle. During that time there was a bird known as a Starling. This bird was not native to the USA and had been introduced from England. Like many animals, when they were brought to this country, they found virtually no enemy to control their population and soon had become a very plentiful bird. They were also loud and sort of obnoxious bird and often drove away the more common and native birds of sparrows and other more desirable birds.

Because of this, Starlings became one that I would routinely hunt for. As a good marksman, you learn that you must always know what is around and near what you are shooting at and make sure there is no collateral damage when you shoot. Continuing, I had become a significant factor in controlling the population of this bird on our farm. I was that new-found enemy that would control the population of this unpopular bird. One day as I was adding to the number of notches in the rifle butt, I noticed several of these birds perched on the electric wire which ran from our house to feed the barn and outbuildings with electricity.

Now, as you get good with something like a rifle, you also build a lot of self-confidence in your ability to hit the exact spot you aim at. As a good marksman, shooting Mr. Starling off the electric wire was an easy and sure shot.

I had done it dozens of times before. So, ready, aim, fire and down comes…you guessed it, the electric wire. Severed just as neatly as you could possibly do it. Now, recall my earlier lesson that fear is a great motivator. Well, I was scared beyond belief. My father, at that time, worked in town and was not due home for over two hours.

I also had no experience with electricity and only enough knowledge to know that it could hurt you badly and perhaps even kill you.

So, I went into the house to tell my mother of my mishap. She was immediately horrified and even worse, went into one of her over reactions and put the notion into my head that when my father drove into the driveway from work, he would not see the downed wire, he would drive over it and immediately be electrocuted and die. The movies at that time would also sensationalize high voltage and its affects. While this was only 110 volts, my limited knowledge made it as similar to 100,000 volts in my mind.

A young person's imagination can get pretty carried away and I conjured up simply horrible pictures in my mind of my dad and his fiery electrical demise. I never did figure out if my mother was playing with my fears or had an equal misunderstanding of electricity, but at this time she was completely convincing, and I was now faced with the prospect that my earlier actions would ultimately kill my father.

Yes, as I said previously, fear is a great motivator. I immediately begin to ponder how this would all play out. He would drive into the driveway, somehow, he would be unaware of the danger now lying across the entryway. Despite my hands waving and as I watched, he would drive over the wire. I would see sparks, maybe even fire and it would be the end of his life. Oh my, I could not let this happen. What should I do? After what seemed an eternity, I decided to take up a farm pail, place it smack dab in the middle of the driveway, and sit there so there was no chance he could drive into the driveway and proceed any further. Of course, I was about 80 feet from the wire as I did not know the reach of that electrical danger.

So then for the better part of two hours I sat on that pail, I contemplated the horrible punishment I would receive and experienced the most fear I had ever been in until that time. Surely this was about the most extreme thing I had ever done wrong. You know, something so egregious, that it could kill your father if it played out. It is amazing what a young mind can create in his mind as to a disaster of such magnitude and then, whoa, the punishment to follow that would result from the most extreme thing I had ever done. And for two hours I sat on that pail and thought only of these things. Finally, the moment of truth arrived, my father returning home, in his car was approaching the driveway. I immediately stood up.

As he drives into our road the emotions run too high and I begin to cry, almost unable to speak, but I must muster up the strength to stop him from this certain death. He does stop, but now I know I must face him with the truth, and still I am chocking on the words and fear that has completely overtaken me, but I manage to tell him of the horrible incident, and that I must stop him from a certain death. And he begins to laugh. Yes, laugh. I am staring death in it very face and he is laughing.

My father is laughing as my fear turns into complete confusion. How could a man that was feet away from being fried by my hand, be laughing about this? This cannot be possible.

I recall the TV series, _The Twilight Zone_, and this surely must be it, I have entered the Twilight Zone. I am in another realm, of the unknown, the completely bizarre. Well after a few moments of deep laughter, he sensed my absolute terror and confusion. He now explains that the only way he could be hurt was to pick up the wire and hold it and then would need to create a ground to do any damage. Driving over it would do nothing.

He explained that the car had rubber tires and they would not conduct electricity and that he was in no danger whatsoever. In addition, this was only 110 volts and probably not much more than a serious tickle even if he could connect to it.

On that day I learned a lot about electricity. I also think the very major mental anguish that I put myself through on that day caused me to go on in my life and learn much about electricity, so much so that in my early plans for my adult life I wanted to become an electrical engineer or electrician of some type. In later years I applied to UW Milwaukee, School of Engineering with electrical engineering as my desired field of study. Sadly, because of logistics, this never was to happen. As I have stated several times, fear is a great motivator.

Chapter 5: I Learn to Drive

A common thread which I learned from the farm is that with each new phase of life, you venture into greater and greater levels of excitement, greater levels of danger, and greater levels of what you will continue to do throughout the rest of your life. I would have to say that learning to drive was probably one of the most significant events in my life.

I will move back in time a bit and talk about my first experience driving which was around the age of seven.

My children think I suffered brain damage around this time, as no one learns to drive at the age of seven. This only occurs in comedy movies.

But remember, we are back to farming in the late 50s and 60s in rural America. One of the farm field work functions was to till the earth after it was plowed. Plowing would take a section of ground, cut it apart and literally turn it over or upside down in order to prepare for a new planting.

This did two things, it buried the old crop remains such as corn stalks and it did the same for the farm manure, or the waste from the farm animals, which functioned as a bit of organic fertilizer. It would also bring up fresh soil from within the earth, that would have more nutrients available for spring planting. After you plowed the earth, you would disc and drag it to break up the large clods of dirt and level it to be more ready for planting. Remember, unlike today's tractors and farm equipment with GPS navigation and many work saving items, not to mention a much larger size, these tractors were but one generation removed from steam engines and horses.

Back to disking. The process of disking was simple, you start on the outside edges of the field and keep driving in an inward spiraling circle around the field over and over, taking a new swath until the entire field has been disked over. The effect of driving in circles and spiraling inward was to cover the entire field through this process. And yes, even a 7-year-old could do this. Once started, you simply drove in this continuous spiral path watching not to drive over an area already prepped until the full field was complete. My dad would have me sit in the seat and make a couple of rounds in the field to get me started and make sure I understood where to go and then he would jump off quickly and allow me to continue by myself. He would then leap off the side of the tractor draw bar (hitch) he was standing on, getting quickly clear of the machine being pulled and would be off to whatever his work for that day was. My instruction was to drive the tractor until the whole field was disked; then to stop the tractor, by merely reaching down and push in the electrical "on/off" switch to the "off" position.

This would stop the electricity going to the engine and within seconds the tractor and whatever it was pulling would chug to a halt. By the time I was expected to be done, my dad would come back from whatever he was doing.

The first couple times I did this it was a bit scary, but I loved driving, I loved the power and noise of the engine, and I was getting work done, so there was a feeling of much accomplishment. Even when it came to other vehicles there were ways that allowed me to drive a vehicle that these days might horrify people.

For example, to drive the car back to pick up my dad for lunch, it was set up that the car was backed up to its parking spot and was ready to go forward when a trip was needed. For those who are older you will recall the famous shift, "three on the tree".

No, there was not a tree in the car, the transmission was a three-speed manual shift which also meant it had a clutch. "On the tree" meant it was affixed to the steering wheel column and stuck out like a branch of a tree.

To start and stop the car you would leave the transmission in gear and then let the clutch out which would engage the engine with the drivetrain and make the car move. But at age 7 or 8, to reach the clutch would have meant my head was below the level of the dash and I would be unable to see anything. So, what was worked out was that we just left the car in low gear.

This would cause the car to move very slowly when the engine was running, and it would move the car around with no problem. The advantage to this was it moved very slowly so by sitting on a couple of Montgomery Ward and Sears catalogs I could see out the front window, over the dash, and drive from point A to point B.

Being inexperienced, the slow movement allowed me to steer and drive the car safely down the farm field roads. And to stop, you guessed it, you just turn the key off. Stopping and starting meant a couple of jerks and jumps, but the car would stop. You simply had to allow about 10 feet to make sure that the stopping distance did not run you into anything. So, I was literally driving a car at a young age.

Well as time progressed my body grew as did my driving skills. And came the need for speed. Yes, like most young men, I liked to go fast. So, let's go back to the car. It was a 1961 Mercury with a six-cylinder engine. Not very much speed is going to come from this beast, but at this young age, any notch up from 3 mph was exciting. So, within months I learned that driving the car back and forth in the fields, you could get going, find a nice long straight away and make short work of that stretch by reaching the accelerator.

Trick was that you were still blinded by the dashboard, so you had to develop a sense of distance, drive in a straight line, and allow for a slowing down stretch of road to pull yourself back up to see and turn the corner. I am glad my dad did not pay a lot of attention to some of the new alfalfa fields as there were some loops or off-road driving which occurred.

If you missed the 90-degree left hand turn, then you had to take a 270 degree right turn to get you back on the road again or at least make several in process steering turns to get you back on the roadway.

I wonder if that's where the Country Western hit, *On the Road* Again came from? Over the years which followed I had much practice and with ever increasing speeds, and complexity of the maneuver and now a bit danger in the execution, my driving skills improved. And life was great.

As I grew older, I took over much of the field work as my dad took a job in town at a textile plant. One of the best lessons in life I was to learn was that even with basic tools you can continuously improve the way you do things and the speed and rapidity at which you accomplish tasks. Practice and repetition are great teachers.

The farm also taught me that you cannot procrastinate. Wasted time is forever lost.

When the weather is right you do things immediately. One of the more famous sayings in Wisconsin is, if you don't like the weather, just wait a half hour and it will change. I learned that you need to have your equipment ready to go so that when the weather permits, you are in the field working, not fixing something.

Whenever a tool was put away, it was repaired, greased if it needed lubrication, and set up for the next eventual use. I also learned the art of multi-tasking during this time.

If I took our one big tractor and used a double hook up of say two discs (one behind the other), and the larger planting drag (double width of normal) I found that you could literally do double the work in the same amount of time. These lessons have come back to me repeatedly in my life that with proper planning and thought you can accomplish your goals and use multiple tools at one time. This has been invaluable and saved many hours as well as allowing me to accomplish much as I advanced my career.

But let's get back to driving.

My dad loved stock car races and we hardly ever missed the Saturday races at Jefferson Speedway. I have no idea if this raceway still exists today, but I fondly recall many of those Saturday evenings. When we first attended, the track was a clay base, and to hold down the dust, they would sprinkle the track with water. This was always a very different and unique experience as these cars used the concept today called the Tokyo drift. The car literally went around the curves sideways, under power, and with the front wheels steering into the skid or the opposite way you would normally steer this curve. It was like being in one continuous skid sideways as they raced around the oval track. It was amazing. One added feature was that if you were close enough to the track, you got covered in mud. These races were truly fun.

I recall a couple of drivers. One whose track name was 'Spider Web', who raced a modified version race car and set his traction with the power of the car's engine so that as he corned, the inside front tire was fully lifted from the ground. Our old 61 Mercury could not be able to do this, not even close. I am sure I tried it, and this explained our often muddy car, but I also learned to do this in the fields about to be tilled, so that I could cover up the evidence and conceal it.

Recall the first time I drove a car I was around seven years old. As mentioned, the old Mercury was a stick shift which meant two things. The first was there was a clutch that needed to be articulated to engage and disengage the engine and move or stop the car. The second thing was that this was a three speed "three on the tree" which meant that the shift lever was an actual lever that came from alongside the steering column, and you would push that lever up and down and forwards and backwards to select a gear. Up and back was reverse, down, and back was low gear and going forward with the lever, up was second speed and down, third. Now, at the age of seven while my confidence allowed me to drive, but my arm length and leg length did not fully support this process beyond steering the car. I could not reach the clutch and of course also not the brake nor gas pedal. Honestly, I also could not see over the dash of car. So, to correct this situation, my dad, who was very clever, found a use for a bunch of old catalogs and stacked them to raise my body up in the seat.

Young readers may have no idea of what I speak but back in these times there was not TV and worse, there were no computers and therefore no internet. So, stores, at that time being Montgomery Wards, Sears, and

JC Penny, all printed large and very thick catalogs that pictured virtually every item you could buy from them. Just as the internet today allows you to browse and see what literally thousands of items looked like, the catalog allowed you to do the same. Anyway, these catalogs, being 3–4 inches thick, could be piled together and could very nicely elevate an adventuresome 7-year-old, high enough to see over the front dashboard. But the problem remained with the use of the clutch and the shift lever and brake. Easy answer, IGNORE THEM. Yes, ignore them. If the car is left in the lowest gear and you turn the car key to start the car engine, it will start and move slowly without any problem. And sitting on about 5–6 of these catalogs, I could see above the dash and hold the steering wheel while driving the car. Since I was not touching the gas pedal, the speed was slow but about perfect for a seven-year-old.

Then you ask, how did you stop? Again, simply, you just turn off the key, the motor stops and the same low gear ratio that allowed you to start the car and move it slowly, would very quickly stop the car just as if braking. All I had to do was watch and steer while I went from point A to point B.

Now, the above seems rather simple and if you check and find what an old "three on the tree" looks like and operates like, you can easily understand this concept. But, with age comes experience… and daring. I think there was a movie that best summed it up. It was called The Need for Speed. I do not recall how long and how many trips I made at this low-speed drive, but I do recall that our farm roads had two features. They had a number of right angles, or 90 degree turns together with several very long straight-a-ways. Now when you combine the need for speed with youthful intelligence (those are not always compatible concepts) you will quickly know that I did find a way to go faster. This meant holding onto the steering wheel, sliding off the catalogs, and getting my right foot to reach the gas pedal. I also learned a little push gives a little speed and a lot of push gives a lot of speed when it comes to gas pedals. This is a concept that I have been able to maintain all my life.

So, picture me sliding down and suddenly the car gains a lot of speed, still in low gear so not wicked fast but, certainly a lot more exciting than the previous idle speed. The trick of this is to recognize distance with a change of speed, remember the corners, and adjust back slower to turn the corner.

I had to guess as a function of time and velocity (equals distance), just how far I was and when to pull myself up, slowing the car and making the turn. For a young man, this was life at its best, driving, making the car speed up, foot off the gas pedal and able to properly steer making a corner and then speeding up again. It would be many years before I attempted a Tokyo drift mentioned previously, but I was well on my way.

These thoughts come back to one of my many learnings while on the farm. The physics of motion are very exciting and as you learn them, and understand them, and respect them, they will guide you for life. I recall my years in high school and college and the Physics classes I attended. These were complex courses for most people, yet I found them fun and almost easy.

I think it was these very young experiences, the learning and the thinking that made my future as it was for me. Even now as I enter my "golden years" my ability to drive and sense how the car will respond has probably avoided several accidents from happening. I wish my grandson could find an old Mercury and a large farm field to spend time in. I think he is going to need that. He thinks he is evil Knievel at the age of four… no fear.

Chapter 6: Duke and Buttons

This is a strange title to start out a chapter, so who or what is this? These were my two pets growing up. Let's begin with Buttons. I do not recall how old I was when we received him. I do recall he was a kitten from a litter that came from my grandmother. He was a yellowish beige color and typical to farm life, lived in our barn. I did become very fond of him, and he was very tame as farm cats go. One of the issues that farm cats have is, that unless they are vaccinated, they can catch many different diseases, one of those being distemper.

Once that germ or bacteria is present it can come back to affect later generations of cats and is almost always fatal. Because Buttons came from a different location and either had the vaccine or some better immunity, he was not affected by this disease. He did love people and when they were nearby, he was there and looking for someone to play with and scratch his back.

One of my favorite games to play with him was called the claw. If you remember all-star wresting from many years ago, you might recall Barron von Raschke. His signature finishing hold was "the claw". He would soften up the opponent with multiple hits and slams and then take his large hand, which he stabilized with his other hand and grab the person by the head and apply pressure. Because his hand looked like a giant claw, the name was created as his finishing move.

Using the same hand technique, I would face Buttons and threaten him with "the claw" and attempt to grab him before he pounced and attacked my hand. And the more you played with him, the more intense he got. Now, if you were quick and somewhat tricky, you could get ahold of him in such a way that he could not bite or kick and scratch you. And, of course, this would just make him madder and more determined to attack your hand.

He loved this and it was great fun. My hands did get a bit scratched up often by days' end.

For those readers who are farmers and had cats, you also recall one other kind of strange thing they liked to do. They were always seeking out warmer places and places that would be warmer than the immediate surroundings. I think this was a trait of the cat's nature. For example, if a vehicle came in off the road, the warmer tires would be a great place for a cat to seek to be. The cat would literally jump up upon the tire and lay down in a nice warm place and from a heightened location they could view the immediate area.

One day we had a large load of wood delivered to our farm and, typical to farmers, the driver and my dad stood and chatted idly for some time. Knowing the routine of Buttons was to seek out a warm tire, I kept milling about and chasing him away and telling my dad to watch for him. Well, you probably also recall your parents when speaking with other adults did not always enjoy a noisily little kid running around and pestering them.

So, after he disciplined me several times by telling me to go away, to quit bothering him, and he would watch out for my cat, he had me go inside our home.

Now, I am a somewhat obsessive person so while I went inside, I watched from the window to try to monitor and make sure the situation remained under control. Suddenly, the talk was done, the driver was in the truck and pulling out of our driveway. Then suddenly there was my cat jumping to the ground in front of the back tires of this rig. I watched horrified and in pure helplessness as my cat was run over. I will not say more but I was very angry with my father for many a moon. After that time I did not forgive him. But let's move on to a more pleasant time.

Duke was my other pet, and he was a cross between a German shorthair and a chocolate Labrador. He had some of the ticking and brown hair characteristic of the German shorthair. Duke was a pet like no other and one which every young man should have as a part of his life. When a puppy grows up with the owner who is also young, and can match the dog's level of energy, this creates an unbelievable bond.

Now understand the bond between a pet and an owner is always very strong, but when they also share the ability to play and do things together, it is even stronger. Duke was always around and if you recall my earlier chapters, my childhood and my teen years were all on the farm. So, as I would tend to fields, which would also mean traveling around the farm fields, going in circles as you do with farming, Duke was forever there and traveling all those miles alongside me. And when the day got long and hot, and I would need to take a break, drink a bit of water, there would be Duke who despite his size, thought he was a lap dog. Yes, a 60-pound lap dog sitting in my lap like a small puppy!

Duke was a breed with hunting on both sides of his lines of heritage. I recall, I did love hunting and fishing, and therefore trained him for hunting.

Southern Wisconsin back in the 60s and 70s allowed farms to place land into what the federal government called "soil banks" or set aside acreage.

The land was probably not needed and to help maintain crop prices, the government actually paid farmers to leave the land idle. This, in turn, allowed the pheasant population to grow and flourish during that time.

In addition, a neighbor raised a large brood of pheasants and released them onto his farm. But many eventually did migrate over onto our land and for a number of years reproduced in large numbers. Given that I was young and in good physical shape, the style of hunting I did was aggressive. While Duke had an excellent nose, with the considerable corn land that was present, the ability of a pheasant to run rather than fly was easy. So, Duke and I became good runners. We would start through a field and when he got "birdy" which means he was on the fresh scent of a bird; we would take off very fast through the field.

While I may not have been as fast as Duke, nor the pheasant, my reach with a shotgun gave me the ability to still reach a bird and almost always drop it. And Duke learned quickly to lock onto the bird, watch and when I shot, quickly find the bird, and bring him to me.

Those years often produced from 20 30 birds per year. For those who have not eaten pheasant, it is very much like chicken.

Yes, I know everything unknown tastes like chicken, but pheasant truly did, they were a bird and about the same size as a chicken so, the similarity was very close. They also ate corn and grain like a chicken, so the result was a meat very similar to chicken.

One of the hallmarks of a pheasant was their ability to hide or when approached too closely, their ability to run. One of my favorite times to recall was going through a patch of tall grass and then coming to a corn field.

Duke was trailing and my progress through the grass was slow but Duke and Mr. pheasant, once they got into the corn field, was very fast.

So, when the pheasant finally got uncomfortable and burst into the air, he was already at a distance slightly beyond my normal shotgun reach. But I still popped off a round and did see feathers fly and a leg drop. But the pheasant was already in overdrive and simply kept flying just above the corn tops. I am guessing he went at least 300 yards and was in a glide somewhat low to ground and suddenly and completely to my surprise, Duke appeared in a leap of all times, grabbed the bird in mid-air and several minutes later, returned him to me.

This was one of his most proud moments, as he knew he had personally got that bird. And when he received his usual head rub, and much treasured back scratch, he knew just how much I was impressed with him. It was simply a moment of excellence for all.

As I like to share some of my learnings from my farm life, the story of my pets offers several key learnings in my life. First, death is a part of life. This was especially true on the farm.

While the loss of anything does result in grief, it is simply something that occurs. And without warning, without any reason at times, you must simply learn that this is natural, and you will survive it and go on with life.

Similar to this thought, is the function that time does heal all wounds. Recall from my pet cat I was furious at my father. It was many days before I spoke with him. But I managed through this and one day realized that everything else had to go forward in life.

Sorrow and grief are natural, and you do have to manage it, but also realize that death is a part of life. I think like taxes, they say, it is one of those sure things. Life and death do not exist separate from one another. Even more amazing is how our planet renews itself. All things die but new life is always there to spring up immediately and replace what was lost. I will share what I consider my most profound thought later in my writing, but this chapter will have much to do with that learning for me.

Chapter 7: Early Mornings

As I was growing up, my favorite time of day was sunrise. On the farm which we owned, there was a large hill in the back section of the land, and this was one of the highest points in Jefferson County. It was about a half mile from our house but even in the dark, it was not a bad walk. With our farm field roads and paths, there was never a problem making this walk before the sun would rise.

Most of this hill was wooded and was not cleared for farmland due to the steep angles of the hill.

The wood line for this section crossed the crest of the hill and you could see a very considerable distance wherever you looked. To the east there was another ridge about 2 miles away and to the west there was a road visible that was about 17 miles away.

Going to the back side of the woods and looking south there was the Bark River and probably around 10 miles of lowlands and the city of Whitewater was visible in part. With a pair of binoculars, you could sight things at considerable distances.

Back to the sunrise. I would love to wake up early and walk to the top of the hill while it was still nighttime. I would find a stump or log on which to sit and watch as the sun slowly approached the horizon. The colors were red, orange, and yellow, and would be in stark contrast to the dark still all around you and in the sky.

As I would watch, a sudden glimmer of extreme bright light would show just at the edge of the earth. If you watched the hillside, you could at times see the light strike the tops of trees and then work its way down as the sun would rise. The blue sky would transform the darkness into even greater color and contrast.

A part of the hill that was only growing in grass would burst into bright green as the sun made its way into full view. I really cannot say why, but this was so completely inspiring and beautiful that I simply sat and watched in awe. I would think of all the physical and astronomical things that were all happening in those moments. It was during these times that I developed what I feel is my most profound learning. Now, I will probably really anger a large number of true Christians with what I am about to describe but this is my true conclusion. I do not believe in a God as we teach in church. I believe that God is good. I believe that God is our universe.

All things good, the planet, the sun, the universe, everything there is, is to me God.

While this is my concept of God, I do see a real purpose for religion, and in my form of belief, I can accept all forms and beliefs of religion. I was brought up Methodist and confirmed as Catholic to marry my wife. But rather than the spiritual Heaven and Hell, I simply believe that your afterlife is the result of what you have done while on this earth.

It is the results of your actions in your life and the things that continue after you die that constitute your afterlife or what we call "Heaven." And then the earth becomes Jesus, the son of man (God).

You need to cherish it, preserve it, and make sure you do positive or good things, not destroy it. The bible provides a comprehensive set of values and behaviors which define how we should best conduct our lives. Religion in all forms does the same thing for all peoples and simply becomes your guide to life. Buddhism, the Jewish faith, all others, have the one element in common, you do good things within humanity, and define how we should properly live our lives. And just as the earth has the immense ability to heal itself, we are given a never-ending ability to adjust our path and live to support Jesus, our earth and all our fellow beings. We can be forgiven and go forward in positive measure from any point if we adhere to these teachings. The earth heals itself and God forgives us and does so forever.

Going just a bit further with my thoughts, our heavenly life after death is not some ongoing form of existence such as heaven in some mystical spiritual place such as on a cloud or some other dimension, rather it is all the things we have done and their ability to continue to have a positive impact and to create more good results.

Persons who have made positive contributions in society leave a legacy and a lasting impact that lives on beyond that person's physical presence. Similarly, hell becomes the composite of all the bad things we have done and how it continues to result in negativity, or pain and suffering of others. Repentance comes at that time when you may have been bad or negative, and you change and do good things from that time forward. And our great planet earth is the base we are placed upon and make these daily choices.

One more time back to that sunrise, it all simply is beautiful, as beautiful, and as fulfilling as you will allow it to be within your life. This is my most complex and profound learning from my farm life.

Religion to me is a guidebook to how to live a proper and good life. With this simple concept, I can accept all religions as they direct their followers to leading a good life. They may have different ways in which they celebrate the religion but basically most come back to expect the good of a person and good as it relates to society.

Even more profoundly, I can accept death, hopefully knowing I have done good things for the most part and then melding with my belief that your life after death comes from the ongoing impact that your actions that continue to contribute after your death. These two things guide me and direct me as I continue through life. This is all part of how I came to view our universe as synonymous with God.

you could get a learner's driving permit and be driving at 15 ½ years of age. I was also working at Eagle Food Store around the same time, so I had money.

In 1966 I purchased a brand-new Ski-Zoom. It was built in Canada by a firm named Auto-Technic. It was a bit advanced at that time in that it already was using a full aluminum tunnel/frame and a center driven track like Yamaha. The engine was a 440cc Sachs, built in Austria/Germany. It was 45 horsepower. The clutch was a very simple block clutch.

A block clutch is basically two steel drums built angled and the blocks were wedge or V-shaped. A large spring would hold the two steel drums apart and when you would apply the throttle, the spinning centrifugal force would cause the wedge-shaped blocks to push on the two steel drums and force them together to engage the drive belt.

Even more impressive, as the machine went faster and faster, the speed would push the blocks ever further together into the two steel drums and act like an automatic transmission to increase the speed of the machine. This machine was capable of a wicked 55 mph.

The suspension was called an opposed "bogie wheel" system. This meant the track sat on top of a number of little wheels called bogies which held the machine up and allowed the track to go around and move the sled.

Now, you recall my early love for snowmobiling. Well, with the bogie wheeled suspension, you could drive this machine on any surface even pavement, and you did not need snow.

The front of the machine sat upon two wide metal skis with a metal bar in center to create a steering function. For the front ski to slide and steer, a bit of snow to bite into was best. So, when we had a cold evening and the next morning the grass was covered with frost, that's all I needed to go snowmobiling. Up and down our farm field roads, across the hayfields, and all over. It was great fun. I had this machine for many years.

Now as this sport progressed, the need for a greater range of travel was soon apparent. In the neighborhood in which I grew up, just about all the farm boys had some brand of snow machine. So, we began by joining our farms together, simply by opening the barbed wire fences, cutting away excess brush and trees, and we created a trail system. Of course, the idea was not unique to our local boys, and many farms began to open and full trail systems were soon established.

We would often go as groups for longer rides. And as the age of "adult" was 18 back then, we also discovered a great place to stop was at a bar. You could warm up and even enjoy a beer or soda. These were great times, and we had a lot of fun.

What is the old saying, "Boys will be boys"? Yup, besides the fun of riding there was the age-old burning question of whose sled was fastest.

So, as we went on rides, we took often ended up with a long straight farm field which also served as a drag strip. Back and forth, most sleds were equal so a good traction start might mean a win. I recall one late afternoon we had opened a new segment of several farms and were out for a ride. And there it was, a beautiful long field and straight for as far as you could see. And there was the sudden roar of these semi-muffled engines, and we were tearing across the field in race mode.

Now, this day, I was a bit behind, I had the throttled pinned and was watching a tree line about a quarter mile away which was the finish line. So, I was fixed on that tree line when I noticed that the other racers veered a bit to the right. This was my chance; this turn had slowed them a bit and a straight line to the trees was the shortest distance and I would win. So, head down to decrease the wind drag and throttle pegged, I was simply flying across the field. Suddenly the word flying took on a whole new meaning, there was a gravel pit near the end of field and the reason the other fellows had deviated was to avoid it. I had not and suddenly found myself about 15 feet above the now much lower earth. Well, once you are in the air, there is very little to do. I recall you do say to yourself, "OH SHIT", and simply hold on for what is coming.

Touch down, no, not football, but like an airship coming to earth. It was a solid hit and about all I remember was holding on and then bouncing up and off the seat but still with my hands on the handlebars. As I came to a stop, the snowmobile was still upright, still running and the only thing different was that the lower part of my body was dragging behind the sled lying face first over the seat, not on it. I broke nothing but do recall several very large bruises on my thigh, and stomach areas. It was a long time before I raced again, and I always checked out the whole raceway from that time forward.

As time passed the sleds got bigger and better. As I grew older my love of snowmobiling never really waned. And as time progressed from the mid-sixties, the number of companies producing sleds went from about 140 to 4. In that time technology improved dramatically as did the speed and reliability of these machines. Progressing through this part of my journey, my next machine after the Ski-Zoom was a John Deere JDX8. This also had a 440cc engine and was fan cooled but developed closer to 60 horsepower and accordingly was faster.

It would go nearly 70mph and used a suspension called a trailing bogie wheel. Same little wheels but the ride was much smoother and quieter. It was a nice sled, and I rode that also for many years. The only remarkable thing I recall with this sled was one day my cousins were visiting and they brought their sled, a 440 Ski Roule. This was manufactured by Coleman, was very sleek and to be honest, not very fast. Old John Deere won every race, both drag and in circles. It was never a contest.

Now, a number of years later, as I then had more of a real job, I could afford the even bigger and better sleds. In the mid 1970's many companies began to offer free air sleds. No fan, but rather cooled by the air flowing across the engine fins, hence the term "free air". These sleds took their beginnings from the race sleds of this time. The free air allowed for more cooling and therefore more horsepower. At the time of around 1976 I purchased an Arctic Cat El Tigre'. This was a 500cc engine with big fins for cooling and if I recall, around 80 horsepower. It was very quick and would top out around 80 mph. I also started to take the sled to new areas via trailer. I recall one trip to Eagle River with a friend who was my local dealer.

Howard Sweno was a very nice gentleman and great mechanic. We did a similar trip for two years and really had a lot of fun and a lot of great riding. I recall one day we chased a wolf down a trail for nearly a mile. Beautiful animal and so perfect in his movements.

On this same trip I recall Howard and I passing a bottle back and forth between our sleds. Kind of more aggressive and riskier riding, but we were a bit wilder and with a new Tiger, we had to be macho. One evening we were riding and trailing at high speeds and driving side by side on just a regular trail.

A regular trail is just two sleds wide. We had worked out that when we met another sled coming the opposite direction, the rider on the left would slow and pull behind the other, and the rider on the right would speed up to allow the other person sooner to pull in behind. Well, mix this with a bit of drink and we were traveling fast. We came to a hill and traveled at speeds to be a bit airborne at the peak.

The problem was, we did not notice a sled coming from the opposing direction. I do not mean to brag but hitting that hill at a high speed, and realizing you are about to meet another sled, and being two wide on the trail, you must perform some special and very fast maneuvers.

And we did. Howard hit his brakes in response despite being on the right side, so I had to do the opposite and speed up to drive in front of him.

But recall the hill. Upon topping the hill, I had to deviate slightly back into the right and jump the front of his sled to miss both him and the approaching rider. I think I had about 2 feet of air and probably about 20 feet distance but managed to miss all, touch down and just keep right on riding. I am sure we scared a decade of years out of the person whom we met. I know for both Howard and me, we trembled and had to pull over a bit to calm and give kudos to each other for living through the event.

Sadly, I note that about one year later, Howard was trying out a new Cross-Country Cat and caught the edge of a plowed farm field. This put his sled into the air, flipped it upon him and while he lived through the crash, he died about a month later from ongoing complications. This was a pretty big shock, and I gave up sledding and sold my 2 machines at that time and went a number of years without.

After a number of years without a sled in about the mid-1980s, I did decide to sled again as I really did miss this sport. I started anew with a Ski-Doo Mach I which was a great sled. At this time the fast sleds were now cooled by liquid cooling.

Better cooling, much more dependable and much greater horsepower. There is not much excitement during this time as I did a lot of sledding, joined a couple of clubs, and rode normal styles of riding. A couple years later I went to a triple cylinder engine, a Polaris XLT (extra light triple). This was also a good machine, but I had one goal in life at that time, I wanted a 100mph plus machine. Both the Mach and the XLT got me to 100 but not over.

My final jump in the speed category came from an Arctic Cat 600ZRT. ZR was the race platform and T was for triple. This was even what they called a triple-triple, meaning 3 cylinders and 3 separate exhaust pipes. This allowed the engine to breathe much better and really produce some high horsepower and speed. My first couple of rides had to be break in so no full throttle.

Then the time came when I hit around 500 miles and it was time to test what this machine could really do.

My ride this day was about 10 miles of trails and then onto a lake. I recall the lake was Pike Lake just south of Park Falls with about a three-mile-long pass.

I drove across the lake just to see if there were any bad spots, clumps of ice or bare ice as each can have a devastating effect with high speeds. All was good. So, with about a nearly 3 miles straight stretch I began to get into the throttle. Off the line this sled could pull the skis right off the ground and hold them there for a hundred feet or so. And then it just kept climbing up. OMG, the numbers by 10s just kept going up. At around 90 an even more amazing thing occurred, the gas shocks and suspension leveled the bumps right out and it felt as if I was on a freeway. So, I pinned the throttle and went for max.

100, then 110 then 115 and about 117 is where I think things were about at max and I was squatted down below the windshield to reduce air drag and wow, I was flying. As I neared the end of my run, without appropriate thought, I sat back up and was nearly pulled right off the back of sled. I had to re-grip the right handle and hold on to pull myself below the windshield to keep from falling off. But wow, what a rush. I tried one more pull across the lake and was able to duplicate the speed. I can only tell you when you are sitting only inches above the ice/snow, this kind of speed is simply mind bending. It is truly incredible.

There is only one other ride which my memory recalls with a bit of wow. Many years later and now with a 2015 Yamaha Apex, a 1000cc machine with the genesis motorcycle engine. Probably around 160 horsepower, fast but not quite as fast as the ZRT above. I was riding this machine with my daughter's boyfriend and a couple of his friends.

It was new, so for most of the ride I was driving slowly for a proper break in. It was obviously fast, but I just did not allow myself to get into the throttle. We were on the trails in UP Michigan which is an old railroad bed. They are flat, straight, and well-groomed so you can drive at very high speeds. We were traveling around 45mph and spaced well for this trail. On our return part of the trip, I finally decided to increase the throttle for a run and see what this machine would do.

It was amazing, the speedometer was digital and simply climbed up by increments of 10 and very soon I was going 90. But looking up, I saw that the rider in front of me had stopped at a roadway intersection. Normally this would not be a problem except the intersection had a plow push about 5 to 6 foot-high on both sides of trail and the rider had stopped right in the middle of the trail and stepped off the left side of his machine.

My mind quickly goes through options of…hit his sled, damaging both, hit him and do a lot of damage or something else. Then I think, well, I am going to be hurt, I am probably going to ruin my sled with any option I pick, so I decide, take the snowbank and whatever happens at least I would not hurt the other rider nor his sled. From 90 mph, I am probably down to 60, but take the bank of snow straight on.

And to my surprise, my sled climbs the bank and I go over it sort of standing up on the side rails of the machine, and now about seven feet in air probably achieve another 70-80 feet of distance while off the ground and amazingly land using my legs as a shock absorber. I took one bounce and now am back on the trail, and completely fine. It is one of those most incredible times in life when you see possible death approaching but get a miraculous reprieve and walk away to talk about it.

Now I must admit I was scared out of my mind, but almost immediately upon realizing that no one understood what had just happened was just a full stupid move I had just lived through, I used the moment to brag that the fat old guy still had it in him. Yes, I was FOS, but no one ever needs to know this at least until now

Now, you might ask how my upbringing on the farm affected this period of my life and further how this was one of my life's lessons. To begin, I sincerely doubt that had I not grown up on a farm and experienced driving at a very early age, developing what I believe to be very excellent driving skill set, and a very high level of awareness of everything around me, I could not have had these experiences in later life.

The reality of how things work in unison was that these experiences and learnings function to develop driving skills which allowed me to think very fast and with a critical thinking skill to solving problems and responding quickly as any situation presented itself. Ironically, I think these attributes may have been the greatest of all that my farm life helped to develop for my future career. We have many fancy words these days such as critical thinking skills and emotional intelligence, but simply stated, through exercise of your brain and putting together your knowledge and experience, I find a person is best able to respond to real-life situations.

I do not know how you really teach or train people in this but if I can offer a suggestion, as you raise a family, you simply do many things, sometimes even a bit dangerous, and offer the value of your wisdom to your family member(s) and then hope they learn and develop a similar or even better method of using emotional intelligence and problem solving. My last thought is that this process is not an event or several events, it is a journey of continuous events.

You should never stop testing, learning, and experiencing things and always keep a mindset that you desire to learn every day of your life. My farm life taught me and gave me the base experience to build upon in my future years. I have worked to make myself learn from every event in my life and to try to form some takeaway from each of these events.

I admit some may be a bit shallow in value, but they build upon one another, and the additive effect can have a very significant impact on your learnings.

Chapter 9: My First Car

As I grew up, I had many experiences which either happened, or at least had their origins on the farm. Many were my lessons for life. Some are simply funny, and I will share a few of those.

As I moved through my teen years, I of course wanted "things". But things cost money and my work on the farm, while it was certainly productive, was not very financially rewarding.

So, when the time came that I was able to drive and secure my license, I almost immediately took a job at Eagle Food Store. I recall at this time when a young person took driver's education through school, they could receive their license at the age of 15½ when they passed the exam.

Since I have been driving a car for about seven years by this time, it was relatively easy to take the written test and then later the skills test and pass. So, by 15½ I was driving cars. So, let's move to my first car. It was a 1965 Ford Custom. It had a 352 cubic inch engine with a four-barrel carbonator. And about 78,000 miles. Now in today's world 78,000 miles is not much but in the 60's era, it was near the end of life for a normal car. Because of the 4-V carb, it also had dual exhaust pipes. While this may sound great when comparing with today's engine sizes and horsepower, this was not a race car. But for me, it was as close as I needed. A good imagination is a great thing.

I of course liked to drag race. The interesting feature of this car was when the 4-V carb would open (or go from 2V to the full carburetion of 4V, so would the oil which was sucked up into the cylinders and created a considerable amount of white smoke out of the back of car.

While street outlaws created the white smoke from spinning tires, mine was more like fogging for mosquitos but with engine oil. Fortunately for me, I was always in front of it. Yes, I did win the few drags races I was in, but I was rather sharp and most of my friends could only afford a 6-cylinder engine, so, they were generally easy wins.

One of the interesting things about this car was that you could flip the air cleaner cover upside down and it would still function against the top of the air filter. The interesting result was that it would create a substantial rumbling noise which would make the car sound a bit "tougher". And at that time, anything that made something louder than normal, this was good. For me this was a hot rod.

So, you might wonder, with these experiences, how were my driving skills? I guess it would go without saying but I was a good driver. I understood the dynamics and physics of a large metal object moving down the road. Having driven in dirt fields and sometimes in snow covered fields I could also negotiate spins and slides and knew the techniques of counter steering in a spin out. And I also liked speed.

My close friends and I would perform a stunt we called rat racing. Two vehicles were involved, and the goal was to drive away from or lose the other vehicle. A friend with another car would attempt to lose me or vice versa. Of course, this would involve a high-speed take-off and some possible dangerous maneuvers.

The main idea was, whoever got in front, would attempt to stay in front and drive to the type of roadway which their car was best suited for. This would give them an advantage and hopefully allow them to stay in front. They would then be in the lead with the other car chasing you.

I had five main friends, Tim, Dell, Ron, Jerry, and Randy. Tim had a newer Volkswagen Beetle, and Dell had his parents 4 door 1957 Chevrolet. The Chevrolet was a 6 cylinder. So, most of the time, it was a follower.

Tim, on the other hand, with his VW had a definite advantage in town. While this car was by no means fast, it cornered exceptionally well as compared with my Custom. The Ford was large and cornered very poorly. So, in the rat race, Tim always attempted to stay within the city and around streets with many corners, while I attempted to get out of town on a long straight country road.

Remember the key was the takeoff, so if a racer could somehow jump in front, Tim would be doing our racing in town, and if it was me, we were heading straight out to the country. I do remember the in-town chases and taking corners which would make the big old Ford almost roll over. It was not meant to be a race car and its performance handling was non-existent.

So, it all came down to a combination of daring and deceit. Daring as you would have to take many a chance of hitting something, losing control, or simply breaking something on the car. Deceit entered when you would drop back, drive slowly for a fair distance, and then watch for a longer straight away, put the pedal to the metal and try to surprise the other driver when he could not accelerate or turn quickly enough not to be passed. And when that happened, out to the country as fast as I could go.

I do remember our in-town driving. Our town's population was only around ten thousand people. The main street length was 10-12 blocks long.

This resulted in a driving route which would at both ends come around and you would double back on Main Street just going the other direction. This was called "running the circuit". I think that is self-explanatory. So, we would be running the circuit, watching for the police to see if we were rat racing or simply trying to stay close to each other. If we would get separated, Tim liked to take his car into a parking spot along the street, parking with the curb side tires up on the sidewalk.

As we would drive by, he would blow his horn and pull out in front of or beside my car often scaring the "heck" out of us. Well one night, as we were running the circuit, Tim did his famous hide and seek routine. The only difference was a city police car was just beside me about a car length back.

So, when Tim went to surprise me, the surprise was on him. He came within a foot or so of hitting the squad car and of course when he saw him, I am sure he left a stain in his underwear. My passengers and I, well we almost stained ourselves from uproarious laughter.

I still remember the OMG look on Tim's face. It was priceless.

So, now let's jump to one of those times when I got in the lead. Because of our work times and school, almost all our shenanigans occurred after dark.

On one particular night I was able to gain the lead and we were tearing down a back road near my country farmhouse.

Tim's VW would max out around 70 mph so when we were racing through the countryside, my goal was to drive at about 75 to 80. And of course, watch his headlights from a distance in my rear-view mirror. I do recall one night when we were racing down Schmidt Road. Not that the road matters but anyway, I was tooling along at about 75 and a cat ran out from the ditch in front of my car. At this speed and it being nighttime, there was not much warning until you realized this was an "oh-shit" moment. The cat went right under my cat with a clunk.

Now I know this is not funny but from Tim's car it appeared the cat was doing a very impressive cartwheel as he proceeded down the road. I was horrified while the pursuit car was completely impressed how a cat would do a cartwheel. There is probably very little learning I could take from this event other than how two people could see the same event in such vastly different perspectives. One almost crying and one laughing. I guess you could conclude also that speed kills.

There is one other memorable event this car participated in. My sister was about 15 months younger than I and when she started driving and she learned in the '65 Custom. She was also more of a social person than I was, so her driving was generally for a meeting with friends and often resulted in her returning home very late in the evening or nighttime. On one night, she noticed that the brakes had failed on the car. Now, I am not going to be sexist, but the female persuasion does generally not have as much automobile mechanical knowledge as the male type. When the primary brakes fail there is an item called the emergency brake which is purely a mechanical link between the driver's left foot and the rear brakes on car.

On this evening the primary brakes on the car had failed as she was driving home. She overshot the driveway and had to make a loop at the end of our road but finally did make it into our driveway.

Now, an experienced driver would simply have applied the emergency brake and stopped, and all done. She forgot about the emergency brake and decided she should park the car close to the garage. So, as she drove up to the garage, she just tapped the gas a bit and aimed for the center of the garage. And of course, the car lunged forward and with no brakes, right into the center post of garage between the two overhead doors. And this is not the end of the story. In recent weeks at that time, we had had someone egg our house.

And the garage was connected to the house structurally, so when she struck the house, there was a giant bang and the whole house shook. Being ready for the egg perpetrators, I had my pistol loaded and ready to go. To make matters a bit worse, after my sister struck the house, she decided she should back the car away from the spot of the impact. This to me appeared to be a hit and run in progress.

So down the stairs I ran with a gun in hand ready to stop the perpetrator. She, now already completely shaken by these events, and as I emerged from the house with a gun pointed at her and screaming at her to stop, I am sure all this completely scared her beyond belief. She never admitted to it, but I suspect she may also have soiled herself that evening.

So, the old 65 Ford does hold a lot of memories, and a possible nightmare or two also. I guess the final learning here was the ability to drive and drive well.

Growing up on the farm I learned the many dynamics of driving a motor vehicle, and certainly a lot of mechanical and related auto repairs. And best of all I had a lot of fun doing all this.

Chapter 10: My First Job

While I grew up on a farm and certainly was a job, I also sought to earn a real income.

My father would pay me two cents for each bail we would handle, and this was from mowing the hay, down to the time of placing it away into the barn. Typically, we might put up or produce 6000 bales of hay annually. This translates to $120.00.

Imagine working extremely hard for about 6 months and getting $120.00. This often included a 12 to 14-hour workday. I guess one of the few positives from this was I did grow to respect earnings very much, and this fact gave me a very strong work ethic. But when it came to money, that wasn't the case. A wage of $120 even back then did not buy very much. When I started driving, I almost immediately sought out work beyond our farm environment so I could earn more money. Several of my high school friends worked at a food store chain called Eagle Foods. Then at about the age of 16 I took my first "real" job as a stock boy at the pay rate of $2.05 per hour. Now, as I look back, that was not much, but a forty-hour week produced almost the same paycheck I worked for most of a summer for. So now I had money to spend and could live a life of riches and wealth. Well, that might be just a bit overstated. But let's talk about my job at the grocery store.

Because I was in school at the time, I would work a combination of evenings and weekends to generate a total of 40 hours. And this time of my life was good. I did work with several friends and even one of them, after several years, became my Brother-in-Law. Yup, I still like to say I found my sister her life mate. But back to the store. As a night stock crew employee, we basically took many large boxes of foodstuffs and placed the individual items in each section of the store and onto the shelves. This also included ordering the food as a section would get low, rotating the food, and making sure as much of the shelves were full as space would allow. And recall most of the night stock crew were high school aged boys. And you know, boys will be boys. We came up with an unbelievable number of things to do. Let me share a few.

In the wider aisles, we would take two grocery carts, and one of the crew, usually a smaller person, would get into the cart where the groceries normally lay and sit. Another, usually the bigger, stronger person would push the cart down the aisle, and we would race. Now this may not sound so unusual or so peculiar, but add another twist, that to win, a racing cart might end up pushing the other one onto the food shelves all the while a human being is hanging with legs and arms outside the cart. This was done about as fast as we could run and, yes, and with many different foodstuffs including glass bottles and bags on these shelves. The race at times was more of a demolition derby than a true race. And we were strong, young, and very determined to win. Recall we were all males. I do recall often spending more time cleaning up on an isle than we spent putting food onto the shelves. I do not recall anyone ever getting hurt but I do know there was spoilage or loss of foodstuffs. There was also a fair amount of clean-up time that took up a part of our work evening. Yes, indeed, I have always thought cart races should be considered an Olympic event. It takes strength, coordination, speed, cunning, a bit of treachery, and a very competitive spirit. Yes, an Olympic sport.

But that was the least of our clever and impressive feats. We had liver fights. This would involve taking a small chunk of liver and throwing it at someone just so it might hit them in the face where it would stick. Yes, a slice of liver will stick to your face for at least a moment. Even a nanosecond is an eternity with liver sticking to your face. I do remember one night when the liver fights got a bit out of hand and several pieces of liver ended up hitting and remaining on the ceiling of the store. This was a rather large domed ceiling, so there was no way to place a ladder to reach the liver and it would need to remain there until gravity finally won the sticky battle. Sometimes, this was the next day.

Frank and Bob were the store Manager and Assistant Manager. While Bob usually gave us a lecture, and then with some laughter, could never really be taken very seriously; Frank, on the other hand, was much shorter, Italian, and had a very nasty temper.

While none of us ever ratted on one another, we would all catch a hell inspired lecture and would be threatened with our jobs. Frank wanted us to believe that our very existence was dependent on keeping our jobs and even more so, that he completely therefore controlled our lives. We were intimidated and usually went back to work, and remained proper at least until the next night.

Now, as I am much older, I think back that this little guy had no idea of what went in the store and would have suffered a heart attack if he even was aware of a fraction of our antics.

I realize that if he had fired us all, the store would have been in one serious world of hurt with no stock staff. So with hindsight, I have a much better understanding of the seriousness ofwarning people, and an even better understand why it never resulted in any true action upon anyone. But if employees think you are serious, it is all that is needed. Fear is a great motivator. It gets you to do things.

I remember another evening when I was working on the sugar and flour aisle or bake goods section. One of the other staff had transgressed into my aisle and this had resulted in a flour fight. Yes flour. It is harmless but ends up needing a lot of cleaning up. The fight done; I had cleaned up my aisle from the floor to the shelves but forgot one key location the side of my face from which to remove the flour. I recall Bob that evening, coming into the store, doing a walk around to inspect that we had stocked up and faced up our aisles. As he walked by, he simply stated, "Johnson, you may want to wash the flour off your face before Frank gets here". Very casually and not even breaking a smile he continued his walk. And believe me, I cleaned up as fast as I could. I knew that hell has no fury like an angry Italian Manager.

On yet another evening, we had a Nair fight. If you do not recall or remember Nair, it is a cream depilatory, and the name came from a shortened version of *No Hair*. When this product was placed onto hair, it would later cause that hair to be completely removed. That evening I was stocking the frozen goods section.

Frozen was basically like every other food item except you stored inventory in a giant freezer with shelves to hold boxes of frozen items. Another worker on the night stock crew, Greg, was bothering me, and I ended up covered with whipped cream sprayed by him onto me and the freezer walls. Once frozen this was very difficult to clean off. So, in retaliation, I got a can of Nair and went after him. Now, the deception of this was that he thought it was also whipped cream in a foaming type of can, so he did not remove it immediately from his face and arms. After about 30 seconds of contact, it will cause the hair to simply fall out sometime afterwards. All I will say is that a guy with no eyebrows really looks funny.

What was even more interesting was that Frank, on the next evening, was hollering at us for leaving our storage areas messy, such as whipped cream frozen onto the freezer wall and several other infractions. The entire crew was lined up and Greg, as the lead stock person, was at the very head of the line. The rest of the crew were near convulsions trying to keep back our laughter while Frank continued his tirade. While it was very difficult not to look, we had to keep from looking at Greg's face with no eyebrows. Mighty tough not to laugh. But we all knew that laughter in the midst of Frank's lecture would surely have provoked an even greater response. I still smile thinking back to those days.

Another duty of the stock crew was to bag groceries at the checkout lines. This would be done at the regular store hours and usually at a time when there was a fair number of customers in the store shopping. And of course, back to the boy's will be boy's thing, we came up with many ideas on how to spice up our work atmosphere. To name a few, the meat department had a phone which was separate line from the front of the store. We would go back into the meat locker and call the front of store. This would get a cashier, who were generally female and ask for some of the following: "Do you have Walter Raleigh in a can, when they came back with "yes", our response, well, let him out". "Do you have chicken legs, response, how do you walk"? My all-time favorite was to call the front, state "this is Mel Hoff, is my brother Jack there, please page him to the phone". It was hard to keep packing groceries as the office girl would announce over the loudspeaker "Jack Hoff to the phone please, Jack Hoff to the phone". Even the more seasoned checkout ladies seemed to understand that one and would enjoy a laugh at a new employee's first day.

One other classic prank was to take a condom, unroll it, press it kind of together and place it around a medicine cup with an Alka-Seltzer tablet inside the condom. The medicine cup would have water in it. You place the ring of the condom over the medicine cup keeping the pill separate from the water. We would then casually walk by the checkout register, set the whole thing next to a check out girl, and press the tablet into the water. And the most amazing thing happened, there can be nothing much funnier than watching a condom suddenly come to full life, spontaneously all on its own. And right next to the checkout lady. Since this was a drop and run prank, only the checkout lady remained with the customer. One or two got hysterical and most got angry. It was always a surprise which we would get. Probably the calmest yet funniest response was from a very nice lady named Sandy who merely stated, "I think it likes me". I had to leave the packing area for a moment on that one.

We did have a lot of fun and this being my first job, it is still by far the most memorable of all that I have done. Oh, and my sister is still married to this stock guy named Tom. While this job was not the farm, the learning that it brought to me did directly relate to the farm.

Had I not worked for the several pennies per bale, I most likely would not have sought other work at such an early age. I did grow to appreciate the value of my earnings; I grew to learn that hard work is often its own reward and I still have cherished memories of this time and the many events that occurred. And I have Tom, my brother-in-law. My experiences and learnings from the farm and this job gave me an appreciation of the rewards of hard work. It gave me an appreciation of the levels of learning that would advance my life in later years, and it helped me to develop a value system of frugality and saving for the future. These attributes have made my golden years a bit more golden.

Chapter 11: Howard Young Miracle Center

For any reader who knows of this facility, they will recognize that the true name is Howard Young Medical Center (HYMC). It is in northern Wisconsin. I started my employment there on January 2nd of, 1979. I moved from an apartment in north Milwaukee and started a new job on the second day of the new year in 1979. I rented the right side of a two-unit townhouse. This facility, in Woodruff, Wisconsin, during the winter is bound by lots of snow and plenty of cold. My next-door neighbors were a young family with two small children, one large dog and a cat. There is much to this time, but let me begin with my neighbors—specifically, the cat.

As the story goes, my neighbor was a pot-head. He very early told me to watch out for the cat because the cat had issues. He described several nights when he had been smoking pot and must have held the cat and blown pot smoke into the cat's nose. I suspect it may have been more than just marijuana. His reason to caution me was that the cat had had a bad trip and must have suffered some form of mental breakdown. After those encounters, he stated that the cat would climb up on the roof of the townhouse and stalk whoever was coming into the building. At the time of my move, there were probably two (2) feet of snow on the roof, so I never saw the cat nor witnessed this event in my first months there. But as Spring came, one day, someone came to my door, rang the doorbell, and was suddenly ambushed by a cat. And, indeed, he jumped from the roof above my doorway onto the person's head. He was in an attack mode. So, I learned to watch the roof and be careful about an ambush. I am guessing, given several other attacks at doorways, the sudden disappearance of the cat probably meant an untimely end or a long ride somewhere. And there was no longer any need to worry about the hopped-up cat.

Next comes the other pet, the dog. Unlike the cat, the dog was amiable and often left surprise packages on my side of the lawn. But this was not his main problem. He liked to chase deer. And being up north in a wooded area, we had plenty of deer. So, it was rather common to see the dog take off after a deer and disappear for a time. On one occasion, a game warden stopped at the house and warned my neighbor to keep his dog leashed or bad things would happen. By now, you have probably realized my neighbor was pretty laid back and, more so, careless. So, he ignored the warnings. Weeks passed, and a game warden again stopped by the house one day. He rapped on my door, I responded, and his question to me was, "Is this dog your dog"? I replied, "No," and he then asked if he was the neighbor, to which I responded, "Yes." He walked to the next door, drew out his gun, and promptly shot and killed the dog. I was aghast and asked what was going on, to which he responded, "he had his final warning about his dog chasing deer last week." He got in his car and drove off. Several hours later, my neighbor appeared at my door, asking what happened. I explained that the game warden had come by, noted the dog was chasing deer again, and that he shot the dog. While I did not own a dog, I did feel sorry for my neighbor but also noted that he had been warned and the DNR would not accept a dog chasing deer.

You might think these two events probably made a complete set of strange and horrifying events. But there is more. One night I could hear the couple next door fighting. The living rooms were back-to-back, and bedrooms were on each outside wall. As their fight progressed, it did get louder, but I am somewhat of a pacifist, so I simply ignored it. That is until I heard a very large bang on the wall and watched as a fist came plunging through the wall just above and to the right of my head. My neighbor, in his anger, had hit the wall and managed to plunge his hand through his wall and my wall into my space. Now, I do not care what you think, but this will scare anyone. So, it did take me a few moments to gain my composure, and without much thought, I stated, "If you do not stop fighting and do not agree to fix my wall, I am calling the police ." Well,

would fly down in two planes. I do not recall the type of plane, I believe it was a King Air, but I do absolutely recall the flight. At the time, I was still sick with the lingering effects of pneumonia and had considerable head congestion. Flying in a small plane comes with variable pressures within the cabin during the flight. I recall chewing gum to try to keep my ears from clogging and helping them to "pop" to equalize the pressure within. Well, this did not work. As we came into Milwaukee to land, the pilot announced that in order to make a timely landing, he had to drop quickly and make an immediate landing. Unfortunately, my right ear would not release. That is until a very major pop occurred, which I believe was my ear drum leaving something damaged within my ear. I did fly down with a Board member who was a physician, but unfortunately, his speciality had minimal to do with ears, as he was a Urologist. And the parts he deals with are not the same parts that were hurting me.

I attended the rate hearing, in pain and without hearing from my right ear. The frosting on this cake was that we were basically turned down and asked to prepare more information and come back again when we completed the additional information, analysis, and data to support our request. It was back to the drawing board. Eventually, we completed the required data, and we did get most of the rate increase we sought.

The end to this part of the story is still coming, however. Going back to my pneumonia, this had developed into some very serious lung congestion, to which I had an almost continuous cough and production of phlegm. I did not state this earlier, but one of the reasons I took a job in northern Wisconsin was my long love for snowmobiling. I did have a snowmobile and, during this whole time, had not bothered to go out and enjoy the snow. One afternoon, I got angry and decided that even if it meant I was going to die, I was going out for a ride, pneumonia or not. The temperature was around 5 degrees F. I suited up and drove off. I do recall the very cold air and that this, with my lungs, really put me over the edge in coughing and reaction. I coughed beyond what I thought I could cough. But, being of Norwegian descent, I was very bullheaded and just kept on riding. I do not recall being out for more than an hour or two; I just recall the coughing. Strangely, as I got home, my lungs were almost clear, and I felt much better. I think I may have broken a slight fever I still had, and I was not as tired as I had been for some time. The best part of this story is my lungs were mostly clear, and whatever I did resulted in my cleaning out my lungs and the apparent end of my pneumonia. I have never tried that again, but I can honestly say that sometimes being extreme can have its advantages. I think there is a contemporary saying something to the effect, "What doesn't kill you makes you stronger." While this learning was not on the farm, the attributes which led me to this action did originate on the farm, so I give the farm life partial credit for it.

Back to my position as Controller. The Associate Director I was working with, Mike, enjoyed his drinks. Over my first six months of employment, two things happened. First, Mike continued his drinking, and he began to increase the amount and frequency of the drinking. As I recall, he was married and had four (4) children. His wife became less and less tolerant of binge-type drinking and even more so of the increase in frequency and amount. The inevitable happened, and he decided to separate from his family. The second of these two things I mentioned above, he decided since I had an extra bedroom and lived by myself in my duplex, he would simply move in with me. Initially, this was not all bad. He had money, and he liked to eat out a lot. So, I enjoyed a rich assortment of meals and restaurants over the next months. The negative of this was his drinking; he did not like to drink alone, so he was very generous in buying drinks for me. This started as only before dinner, then progressed to be another with dinner, and then in the end, one before, one during, and one or two after dinner. Back at that time, I was amazed at how quickly I could build up a tolerance for and enjoyment of alcohol consumption. I remember one day back at my apartment, having a round of drinks after our return from dinner and realizing that I had consumed around 8 to 10 mixed drinks that evening. Having grown up on the farm, this would never be an acceptable lifestyle. I had the good sense to put myself on a complete forbearance of alcohol immediately and, in the next several days, asked Mike to move out as soon as he could find another place. He was understanding and did move out. He moved into a trailer, found a girlfriend, and I now watched from a distance as he destroyed his life. He was my second boss, and I probably worked for him for about 6 months.

My third boss was Dick B., who was the Executive Director. While my position did not change, I now reported directly to the top person. His background was in finance, so my duties remained consistent during this time. Given the loss of my first two bosses, he sought to replace these two Associate leaders who had departed. This may be a rather simple matter, but let me expand on the leadership structure in HYMC at that time. The creation of HYMC came about from a donation from a gentleman by the name of Howard Young. Mr. Young was a New York art dealer and was very successful and wealthy. He would spend his summers in the Minocqua area and was known to be close friends with President Eisenhower. So, he traveled in prestigious circles and accumulated much wealth. The story goes that one evening while visiting Minocqua, he had enjoyed a very large and rich dinner and developed some bowel obstruction. He was rushed to the Lakeland Hospital, where Dr. Henry Ashe, Surgeon, did an emergency procedure and saved his life. Mr. Young was extremely grateful, and he asked Dr. Ashe what he could do to support this facility. He received the reply, "Build a new and modern hospital." After that, Mr. Young donated $20 million to construct a new hospital and establish a trust as part of the donation for later years. Now move this back 50 years to the 1970s and note that this was a very substantial amount of money. The gift was given for half to be used to build a new hospital and half to be held in trust for the future growth and needs of the hospital. And in 1977, a new HYMC was completed.

Getting back to the executive team. The old administrator from the Lakeland Hospital was dismissed, and Mr. Berger was his replacement. There was also a new and very powerful Board of Trustees that replaced the old members of Lakeland Hospital. The Chairman at that time was John S., who ran a consulting firm out of the Chicago area. Dick B. had been in hospital finance and was also in administration at a larger hospital in Florida before his move to northern Wisconsin. He came with a 3-piece suit and an air of importance. In my reporting to him, I had to change somewhat the function I performed and serve in more of an administrative function than just a purely financial one. He was not a uniformly decisive person in my estimation, and the more difficulty the organization got into it, the less decisive he became. I recall one of his worst decisions as he had assumed his role was to terminate the old administrator by the name of Marty Anderson. Marty was well-liked and had built the Lakeland Hospital from its early beginnings. Dick's second poor action was his decision to purchase himself a corporate car. He selected a top-of-the-line Buick and one that was loaded. Coming from the days of Marty Anderson, this was a gigantic and controversial change. Marty had received a rather small paycheck and drove his car. He had been responsible for securing the Howard Young monies, building the new hospital, and was now let go. Dick, on the other hand, now had a fancy car, 3-piece suits, and had problems making decisions. He did make one very memorable decision which I still recall to this day. When he ordered his new car, he was still thinking about Florida, so he did not order a rear window defogger. Being in northern Wisconsin, this was a necessary item, so he had an aftermarket one installed. This was basically a flat copper wire of two strands that wove back and forth in the back window with a center connecting the set of flat copper wires. The only problem was, if you can picture this from the outside, it looked like a giant Dollar sign. While I know his intent was not so, it appeared he was flaunting the cost of the car with a dollar sign in his back window. It seriously even made the local newspaper in articles. One of my favorite sayings became, "dick Dick before Dick dicks you." Because he terminated the much-loved prior administrator, his time was also in short order. Mr. Sheridan acted, and Dick soon came to an end as my third boss.

Almost immediately, a new administrator was found, whose name was Michael S. Mike, a schoolteacher who had a long friendship with Mr. Sheridan. He became my fourth boss. Now, Mike, having no experience whatsoever in healthcare, viewed his job as someone to gather a large check and talk with people. He loved to meet with people and, most especially, to get to know them personally. Very personally. He especially liked attractive young nurses, married or not. What followed was a number of changes in the nursing leadership of those he was attracted to. The joke became that those nurses had to earn the job title of *Head Nurse*. Well, that title had a fully different meaning to him than that of a conventional hospital nurse manager. Yup, Head Nurse took on a very different meaning.

Another of the things that Mike S. did was to look at the organization and, given the absence of a top financial person (I was a mid-level financial manager, with duties focused on Medicare and Medicaid reimbursement and budget, which was why I was hired) he recruited for a top-level finance Associate Administrator. He recruited a senior-level accountant out of the firm of Peat, Marwick, and Mitchell. Very high-end and whose name was Bruce B. Now Bruce was an interesting person; he was a CPA from a big firm and had senior-level experience. However, in a similar fashion to Mike, he had no health care/hospital experience whatsoever. He became my fifth boss. He was arrogant and just a plain nasty person. He had a pet name for each of his staff, and mine was "Dirty Pig Fucker". I soon understood why he reportedly had been pushed out of the CPA firm where he had most recently worked. He was the worst person I have ever had the pleasure of working for. His crass demeanor, his constant belittling, and his course mannerisms quickly convinced me that I was ready soon to move on with my career.

But one more part of this story. This is where things take a very different turn. Remember, my role was in a mid-level financial management position, and I was primarily responsible for the Medicare and Medicaid reimbursement and budget issues. This meant that I worked very closely with our audit firm when the annual financial audit was performed. Dale V. was our audit partner, and over many years, I developed a very long, very positive, and productive relationship with him and the firm. To the day of my retirement, I supported the use of this firm for our audits and accounting needs.

Our fiscal year end was December, and therefore, our audit would be conducted from January through March of the following year. As a custom, at the end of our audit, we held some form of audit party where all who were part of the audit would enjoy an evening of socialization and dining, Back to HYMC, in this particular year, as we completed the audit, we decided to hold the party at my house and build a giant bond fire for all to enjoy. On this one evening, we were well along with our party, meal, and liquid libation. Without an invite, Mike S. showed up and joined the party. And in a similar fashion to the unsavory things I noted above, he began hitting on Katie C., one of the office staff.

While everyone was outside by the bond fire, the food and drinks were in my house in the kitchen. After a while, Katie and Mike decided to go into the house for food and drink. This seemed to be a natural and acceptable thing to all in attendance. I am sure everyone lost track of time, and after probably 20 minutes, a couple of people wanted a new drink, and since it was my house, I offered to go in and get them. I had left most of the lights off in the house, so going into the kitchen with it dark seemed to be without question. Entering, I turned on the lights, and my expression was, "Oh shit." I immediately turned the lights back off and, as fast as I could, went outside with nothing in hand. I did not know what to say, nor did I speak to anyone other than to mumble "Oh shit" a couple more times. Still desirous of another drink, another person shot into my house. And just as quickly came out, also repeating, "Oh shit." This person, however, was able to add, "he is fucking Katie on your sink." Yes, as Paul Harvey would say, that was the rest of the story. From all appearances, they were having sex on my countertop. The group was all very shocked, and no one really had any idea what to do at that moment.

Well, now having been disturbed twice, both Katie and Mike came outside and rejoined our party. The only difference was Katie had a very red face. Now you might think this was the end of the story. And if it ended there, most would conclude this was a pretty spicey ending. But during this same time, Katie's husband had called several times and wondered when Katie was coming home. They lived about 4 miles down the same road as me. After a second call from Katie's husband, she did decide to leave. Recall Mike had arrived last and was, therefore, the last car in the driveway and blocking the end of the driveway. So, he had to leave with Katie in order to get both cars out. The party group had decided to go inside and were in the process of moving into my house. At this point, we concluded that Mike had left, Katie had left, and we were back to a somewhat more normal situation. Katie's husband did call for a third time, and we told him she had left about 4 minutes before and would be home shortly. What we did not know was that she and Mike had got into the back seat of his car, still parked at the end of my driveway. Rather than leaving, they were going to finish what had been interrupted inside my house.

Now Katie's husband, who finally grew tired of waiting, and being told she should be home, decided to come to my house and get her. Since my guests and I were inside, we saw none of the drama about to unfold at the end of my driveway. Katie's husband arrived only to find two cars running and sitting at the end of my driveway. He got out and found nobody in his wife's car, so naturally went to the other car. The two occupants were so busy in the rear seat they never noticed him drive up, so upon his opening the car door (I suspect he could not see in as the windows were all fogged up), there were some big surprises that simultaneously occurred all within the next moment.

Now, remember that my staff and I were inside my house at this time, so we knew nothing of this event.

The next morning, I came to work as normal and was not expecting much to occur that day. I should also mention that Katie's husbands' mother also worked in our offices doing the billing work, so she was a part of my office team also. She was one of my direct reports. As I came in, I asked what was new as I greeted people with a Good Morning. I instantly learned that Katie had resigned, she and her husband were getting a divorce, had separated, and that the family intended to sue the hospital, specifically Mike S., for his sexual proclivity. Did I mention my new favorite term was now "oh shit"? Yes, indeed, this was giving new meaning to what some called HYMC Howie's Whore House.

By now, you must think this is the end, but this story does not end there. At this time, I was still the Controller and was obviously caught in a rather delicate situation. I truly was hoping I could either disappear or people would somehow decide to remove me from this equation of involvement. Several days went by, and I was thinking, indeed hoping, maybe, just maybe, I have escaped this most awkward of situations. Well, not so, as next comes a call from Mr. S, the very powerful Chairman of the Board. He had a deep voice, and with great authority, he invited me to personally come and dine at his house in Lac du Flambeau. Now, as I mentioned above, I am a peon in the hierarchy of HYMC. There can be no reason for this invitation other than to relate to Mike S's actions. His invitation does not really give me an alternative other than to attend. So, comes this night, and I go to his home, not sure what to expect, but I do know that I have firsthand knowledge of these incredible events.

We have dinner. I have never eaten at a 30-foot table where I sit at one end, and the host sits at the other with a servant providing the meal courses. "Oh shit" comes to mind once again. During dinner, I am mostly silent while Mr. S describes some of the work he does. During this self-description, he makes frequent references to the phrase, "and I can make people, and I can destroy them." Based upon my experiences to this point, I believe him.

He then invites me into his cigar room for a cigar which I decline, but he insists I sit down for just one more moment. He concludes with another iteration of how he makes and breaks people and then simply ends with how this has been his pleasure, and he sincerely hopes I have enjoyed the evening and understand all that he has said. I respond with a brisk yes, but still, I am thinking, "OH SHIT,"

Now this surely must be the end of the story here, but there is still a bit more. In the next several weeks, I will start to look for another job and to plan accordingly. At that time, however, I was confronted by my good doctor friend, who flew to Milwaukee with me, the Urologist. He is still on the Board and, of course, has heard much of the rumors flying around about all the above events. He visited my house one evening, and we have a several-hour chat about all this. It was a rather interesting visit as he heard I was planning on leaving, and he made a bid for me to stay and reconsider. Second, he is trying to put together information on these occurrences in his role as a Board member. Recall the theme of my writing is what I have learned on the farm. This kind of stuff just doesn't happen on a farm, but there is one common value I did learn from the farm, and I used it here. Always tell the truth and be brave. Whatever happens, happens. So, I did just that. And what happens next is amazing; the Board convenes a special meeting and, based upon the bylaws, removes the Chairman from his position and then requests his resignation from the Board. Then upon the formation of a new Board, they terminate Mike S. from the position of Executive Director. Oh shit, wow, what a move. Justice does prevail.

Building upon this learning, I do develop better confidence in myself and one where I will not allow others to intimidate me or threaten me in any form. I do what I have come to believe and use all my intelligence to make decisions and then stand by them. It can be a daunting process, but in a repeated fashion, it has served me well.

Back to HYMC. One of the Associate Administrators became the new Executive Director after this shake-up. I now have my sixth boss in a three-year career. Now the story becomes short after this, as about 3 months into this position, the latest CEO abandons his wife and runs off to another state with his secretary. Yes, I could not make this up in my wildest of dreams. But sticking to my plans, I am shortly resigning and taking a new job in Racine/Kenosha area as Director of Finance for St. Catherine's Hospital. Now I suspect you are thinking, yup, you got it; oh shit, what else could happen? This little three-year period of my life has much more to add, so much so that I will devote another chapter to this.

Now you might think, 'Well, that was a lot of activity,' but the best is yet to come. As you will recall, I was still a very young person in my chronology. Upon graduating from college at the age of 20 and then three years of work at Blue Cross, I would be around 23-24 years of age when I moved to the Minocqua-Woodruff area. This was also a time when I was very shy and mostly inexperienced. My next chapter delves into my more personal life at this time.

Chapter 12: My First Love

Going back to my second boss at HYMC, Mike K., he was a social type of person and did a bit of matchmaking. Suddenly I found myself dating a girl who worked in our office and who did the hospital credit and collection function. She was slightly older than me and had been married previously and divorced. She was a pleasant young lady and relatively attractive. They say that in your first love, you tend to fall head over heels in love. Well, I did just that. Looking back, I am unsure if it was real love or just infatuation, but I was hooked and wanted to be with her as much as possible.

I write this chapter separately from my experience at HYMC, although these events occurred within the same period. As you put these experiences together, you can see that this was a very eventful time in my life. To compound this active time, I also found my first true love, who ultimately became my wife. So, there are many sad and also some very happy moments as I recall this time. Remember, I was the Controller at HYMC and just 3 years out of college. And I was single. As most people know, there is no time in life when it is written that you should be married and begin this new journey in life. However, it was a normal time to get married around this age, based on our country's social standards. One problem was that I was shy, and as you recall from my prior job, I was not strong by way of my confidence. Lacking confidence, I also lacked the drive and fortitude to date and seek out a girlfriend. This is where Mike K. enters the story. Besides what I mentioned, he was a bit of a matchmaker.

There was a young lady with whom I worked in the business office. She served as our collection person. She was single, attractive, and had a nice personality. I do not recall the exact manner in which he got us together, but we met and dated somewhat slowly at first. As we got to know each other, we began to see each other more often and more seriously. Her name was Cyndi. She had blond hair and a pleasant sort of round face and was a nice lady. As we dated, we got to know each other better, and everything was correct for us.

Now remembering that I started by stating I was not a confident person. And being in my early 20s, I was also plagued with the very normal infliction of raging hormones/testosterone. Cyndi, who was a few years older, had apparently also come into her time with higher levels of hormones. So, life was good. We were careful, and of course, we did get a lot of advice from those around us. I recall one associate, Art, whose favorite line was "keep it in your pants," and Mike K., who bought us a box of condemns. Mostly all this was done in jest.

We soon spoke of getting married and began to think about what our future would be and what family things we should be planning for. I had always wanted a family, probably two children, and often spoke of that. As I think back, Cyndi never shared that idea but also really never made any negative comments when I spoke of family. We did things together and shared times, and it was a good match. We shared many interests and enjoyed similar activities.

As I mentioned, we also shared several friends. This occurred because we both worked in the hospital and the same department (Business Office), and all of our friends were from this group of people. There was Mike and his girlfriend, Karen. There was Art and Bonnie and probably Cyndi's best friends were Dave and Nancy. Dave and Nancy were different in that both had been previously married, and each had left a spouse to allow themselves to come together and ultimately marry. They were also somewhat judgmental in nature. By this, I mean they would suggest things that each of the two of us should not relate to each other. They would plant a seed and then sit back and let it germinate and occasionally add to it and support the seed of doubt they had sown. While I will never be sure, it seemed in my hindsight that they had planted many a seed of doubt, and either I was blind, or it was not as real as they made it seem. But I noticed Cyndi began to distance herself from me and spend much more and more time with Nancy.

As we continued to date, I had decided to simply allow both of us to spend more time with Dave and Nancy, so one long weekend, it was decided we would go to Saxon Harbor on Lake Superior and camp. I had bought a tent and all the gear, so we were ready. Then our weekend began. Almost immediately, we had a disagreement which, as I recall, related to doing what Dave and Nancy were planning to do, while I wanted to spend some of our time alone—just Cyndi and me. While I do not recall it being a very intense disagreement, I know that neither of us spoke to the other for the better part of our first day there. I compromised, and we spent much of that time with Dave and Nancy.

That evening, as it got late and time to go to bed, we both adjourned to the tent, and I confronted Cyndi with our disagreement, noting we had to resolve it, and spoke about my concerns of just doing as Dave and Nancy wanted and desired to spend time with just her. We had a rather long talk and, after some time, agreed that we should get along and spend some time just for her and me together. And so, we kissed and made up. And we kissed again, and maybe a few more times. Well, I will dispense with further details, but the rest of the evening became very romantic.

The trip became a nice time, and we were very romantic for much of the time until our departure. For me, this seemed like a very beautiful time, and at least for a short time, I suspect it was for Cyndi also. But then that dreaded day in our lives came; she was pregnant. This was an event we had not planned for and were honestly not ready for in our lives. I desired to talk with her and try to work through what we would do. Hers was one of fear. She withdrew from me and would only speak with Nancy. I was hurting inside, as I am sure she was, and I was trying to work by myself while she worked through her thoughts with Nancy. And then, one day at work, she came into the doorway of my office, tossed her engagement ring back to me, and stated, "Nancy and I have decided I should not marry you." I know it is pretty cliché, but "OH SHIT."

Now, I am not sure this will be the most traumatic event in my life; I know now there will be others with much more meaning and emotion, but until this time, this was the biggest and harshest event I had ever been hit with. For the next several weeks, I tried to meet with Cyndi and talk with her, but other than just to spend a moment, she had completely separated herself from anything to do with me. I do not pretend to know the stages of grief. I know there are stages, but I do not know the names, order, or timing in which they occur. For me, I was desperate and hurting in great amounts. I turned inside myself and could not deal with the pain and set of emotions I was facing. I tried to reason but did very poorly in this and became angrier and fuller of self-pity. As several weekends rolled around, there I was, at home, alone and hurting deeply. One weekend as I reached my low point, I decided to make a homemade pizza (which I had newly discovered). It was an interesting lunch that I endured that day. I made a large pitcher of black Russian drink and the pizza. And I took one more item with me, my .357 magnum pistol, loaded and ready. I sat down in a chair on my deck with the pizza, the black Russian, a large glass full of ice, and my pistol. I think my pain was at the point where I understand how you feel that life is not worth continuing. I ate a couple of the pizza slices, drank the full pitcher of black Russian, and became quite drunk. I looked several times at the revolver, thinking this could stop my sadness, but then instead, I tried to stand up, teetered, and fell off my deck over the rail and onto a pile of flagstones piled below. I had been planning to make a lower-level patio with these stones. The fall was only about 4 feet. I should have been hurt, but in my drunken state, I think three things happened. First, I was very loose and fell limply without injury. Even if I had been injured, I would not have felt it with the buzz I now possessed. Second, while I had thought about suicide, the fall, the drop, and the sudden result of all this drew my attention away from that idea. Lastly, I passed out shortly after the fall. Totally and completely out. I do not know how long I lay there in this state, but I suspect for probably at least an hour or so. When I came to, I had the sense enough to determine if I had broken any bones, my skull, or what? Surprisingly, I did not even have a pain spot or bruise that I could detect. I also realized that I was really screwed up, and probably for the first time in my life, I needed to seek the help of others. Serious help, that is. While the farm had taught me to be strong, self-sufficient, and able to handle any situation, love taught me that my mental and emotional pain could be far beyond anything physical I had yet to experience. It taught me that the pain of the heart was probably greater than any other I would ever experience. The loss of someone you love is as painful as it gets.

The above events happened on a Sunday, so the next day, I was back at work. I bit my lip and drew together every bit of courage I had and called the clinic psychologist, Chuck M. Chuck was about my age. Before this time, I had never really dealt with behavioral or emotional issues. Chuck M., I had only known him by name, not by use or experience. So, I mustered up the strength, made an appointment, and met with him for the first mental health hour in my life. I talked about myweekend, my heartbreak, and my desire to try to somehow put an end to my anguish, sorrow, and pain. And we talked. My experience in later life is that mental health issues can be complex, and in turn, they often take many sessions to resolve or secure the help you need. Being a business graduate, I assumed that was more because of financial reasons. If you read between the lines, I was not very much of a believer in therapy, so my thought was once and done. At that hour, Chuck came to suggest I read a book titled Looking Out for Number One. He shared that much of my hurt was the result of seeking my support from Cyndi and, while doing so, leaving myself completely unprotected and emotionally dependent on her to make my life happy. So, I took that book home, and within two days, I read it from cover to cover. I am not sure whether this was the most profound concept I have ever discovered, but it certainly ranks among the top 3 in my life. If you do not look out for your own needs, you cannot properly look out for the needs of others. I was what I call a "caregiver" type personality.

Simply put, I am a person who turns my attention to caring for others but forgets the importance of looking out for himself first. I did not think and manage my needs and expended my energies on others I cared for. My center of values was not making myself strong and making sure my needs were being met but caring for and meeting the needs of other people. I did not look out for myself or properly care about myself, as I was caring for and saving others. In my relationship with Cyndi, I was so focused on caring for her and trying to meet whatever standards or perceived standards she exposed; I had lost focus on my importance and the concept that I needed to care for myself first in order to be strong for myself and maintain my wellbeing. Before I could develop my love and relationship with another person, I had to develop my relationship with myself. I had focused on Cyndi as my life's center and left myself out of the care equation. With my lack of self-concern, I nearly committed to self-destruction. It is a flaw I have had to manage all of my life.

In this writing, this is the greatest learning in my life. In order to care for others, create healthy relationships, and love others, you have to first care for yourself. You must be number one in meeting your own needs in order to have the strength to care for others.

Going back to my farm experiences, I had learned the need to look out for yourself, but somewhere as I grew up and especially in my first romance, I had lost much of this very important concept and value. Having at least thought of ending my life helped me realize that in order to have a purpose in life and to make that purpose great, you must first look out for yourself and make yourself the strongest person you are capable of being. Putting this experience together with my other experiences at HYMC, it was a true time of growth in my life. Growth is painful, but in its end, it is very positive.

To close this chapter of my life, you will recall my opening remarks about also meeting my wife during this time while employed at HYMC. Well, more will come about this in future chapters, but during this three (3) year journey of my life, I did meet a young lady by the name of Mary Elizabeth End, or Mary Beth for short. We met and shared a life together for over 41 years. And now, in the 67th year of my life, she is still my wife and the mother of my three children. Sadly, as I complete this chapter, I note that with her many health issues, she did pass away in March 2021. I like to think all of these events, in some magic way, brought us together and gave us much in our 41 years together. Even more so, I feel that we created much good in the lives of others during these 41 years, and that good is living on through the wonderful and good things which my children now do and through my beautiful grandchildren. They truly personify all the beauty and love this world can hold.

Chapter 13: My Family

The elements of my family include my parents and all my direct relatives, and then from marriage, all my in-laws of varying levels. For this chapter, I wish to focus purely on my three children.

To begin, my first child was William or Bill for short. About the moment Mary became pregnant, I would place my hand on her stomach and say, "Hi Bill," because I really liked that name for a boy, and a boy for firstborn just seemed natural to me. My wife would protest, saying, "How do you know it will be a boy"? My reply always was, "Bill" would be such a funny name for a girl. Therefore, he must be a boy. When that day finally came, sure enough, it was a boy, and he was named William or Bill for short. My choice of names came from very prominent businessmen I had known with the same name, and all this seemed very proper and an easy selection.

Bill's first days were a bit tenuous as Mary wanted to nurse and begin the baby's development the old-fashioned way. The problem was her nipples; they would invert and not allow the baby to be nursed. She was determined and kept trying for several days. This started to become a bit scary since Bill was not eating or receiving any nourishment, and he began to lose weight. This could not go on for very long. After a couple of teary moments, we(she) finally decided the use of baby formula was necessary for him to thrive. With this change, he was quickly growing and doing very well. Recall in other sections of my writing, I noted Mary had multiple sclerosis. After the birth of Bill, she became depressed with problems of unknown origin, initially diagnosed as depression. This became the diagnosis because she had suffered depression in the past, and the symptoms were similar. Also, recall in these times, there was no MRI or any other method to diagnose MS. Doctors simply went to a diagnosis of severe postpartum depression as a rule-out everything else type of diagnosis. To further complicate matters, they felt she needed hospitalization for this. So, Mary was admitted to a hospital for depression.

Remember that thirty-eight years ago, there was no family medical leave. Therefore, I had to continue working or face quick financial distress. To manage this situation, on a weekly alternating basis, my parents, and then alternating with Mary's parents, would come and stay at our house and care for Bill. Each set of grandparents would care for him during the day, and I would care for him at night. This worked well with one exception, on those nights that Bill was awake and needing care, I got no sleep.

Now this is where one of those farm lessons comes in: some of the farm animals are capable of sleeping without laying down. As I think back on that time, I would literally hold Bill, feed him, and then fall asleep with him sleeping on my shoulder or in my lap. I then got a few hours of sleep while he slept all nice and warm against my body. It was sort of a form of bonding. I also developed the ability to function well with 4-5 hours of sleep per night.

As Bill grew in these early years, we also found that Mary could not take care of the three children without some help. Shortly after the birth of Katie, our third child, we moved to Eagle River. Bill was about 4 years old then, and we enrolled him in the Day Care Program at Northwoods Living Care Center, where I was employed. This was a hospital with a multi-faceted set of programs. The program was unique in that the Director of the program, Peggy T., set it up to function more as a preschool program. The timing of these actions was exceptional as this was the dawn of computers. At that time, they were more of a micro-computer such as MacIntosh. Through her many talents, Peggy was able to secure donations for the purchase of an early Mac Computer. So, at age 4, Bill started his career in computers and software management. He was exceptionally bright and had a computer at his complete command. With no one or nothing else to constrain him, he developed his love and ability to understand and work with this brand-new technology. As I attempt to draw on my farm experiences, it is hard to tie my past to his journey other than to say that timing in life, farm and otherwise, is everything. When the opportunity presents itself, you take advantage immediately.

Bill went on to graduate from Stanford with two degrees, one in Computer Science and one in International Economics. And I still credit Peggy and the early use of the little MacIntosh Computer.

A second lesson from the farm would be if you plant a seed, nurture it, and care for it well, it will yield a great harvest and much bounty. So, it was with Bill.

My second child was a girl, Maureen. Similar to Bill, right after her birth, Mary was again hospitalized with depression, but by this time, doctors thought there might be something more than just depression. Her symptoms persisted beyond the treatment for depression. But without MRI, there was still no definitive answer to what might be happening to her. Previously, I was able to work with both my parents and my in-laws and continue my job and build for our future.

Maureen, being the middle child, we had learned to be a bit more hands-off than Bill, our first. She, therefore, developed more freestyle behavior. She was extremely bright but felt life should be taken less seriously. I have always believed that she was the most capable of learning and most intelligent of my three children, but she liked to party and developed into my "I have never missed a good party" child.

With her intelligence, she was able to easily maintain a solid B average and do so with very little work, which meant more party time. Being creative and bright, you can have a lot of party time if you make that your goal.

I will not go into the many parties she attended nor the somewhat tense moments she created, but they were many and most interesting. I do recall one where she left through the back door of the party house, and traveled about 2 miles through a wooded area, in the winter and at night in the dark. She was able to contact the person she had driving her car around so that it was not parked at the party, and as the police were attempting to raid the party, she got back to her car and safely home. How would I know this? Well, when you get a call from the police department at midnight that your car was seen driving around near a party that just got busted, and they ask who was driving the car, and you have no idea where anyone is or what is going on, it does make this a prominent moment. And, yes, no ticket, not busted, and sometime later home safe. There were several of these incidents which I learned of, and I am sure, even more, that I would not know about. Anyway, she grew up fine and managed a bachelor's degree and a master's degree in Psychology. She is now the lead Psychologist at the health care program I worked at.

I digress a bit. The three years I spent in Kenosha/Racine, besides the birth of all three children, was an interesting time for me. I was working in Kenosha St. Catherine's Hospital and was in the position of Vice President of Finance. Related to my recent and present experiences, I knew more and better how to manage a hospital than the present CEO I worked for. Recall my departure from HYMC in that chapter, which prompted my move to Racine, was a significant level of chaos that I had experienced with administrators who were marginally competent. During the next three years working in Kenosha, and living in Racine, I decided to complete my CPA certification and also to complete a master's degree in health services administration. I also think the 5 hours of sleep had something to do with this for two reasons. First, I trained myself to function at a high level of output and to do so with just 5 hours of sleep. Secondly, I had watched a number of Administrators get jobs who seemed to make many mistakes and often needed help with how to handle a situation. I will not detail these events, but during this time, I did complete my master's degree, and I passed the CPA exam. This gave me two sets of credentials and accomplishments to put behind my name. Now, back to the children.

Near the end of the third year, just as we left Kenosha/Racine, along came Kathryn, or Katie for short. Mary, with her health problems, had been advised to have only two children, but like most things in her life, she did not listen, and now number three was on the way. Both of the first two children were born via C-section, so it was automatically planned this would occur for Kate.

But things did not go as perfectly as the first two pregnancies. We knew Kate was small, and this was going to be a more difficult birth. Approximately 6 weeks before the full due date, an ultrasound showed problems, weak heart tones, and other indicators that the baby was in distress. We went to the hospital, and without much wait, Mary was quickly rolled into surgery, and after only a few minutes, Kathryn Jeanette Johnson was born.

Kate was a low birth weight (5 pounds) and about 6 weeks premature. The problem was that her lungs were not yet fully developed to function outside of the womb. Shortly after her birth, her left lung collapsed, and she was placed into the neo-Nate unit and had to have a suction tube placed into her chest to draw the lung back into being inflated. I was gowned and went with her into the neo-Natal ICU.

I have to confess it was nothing short of hell watching the doctor cut and stick a small tube into the side of her chest and hook a vacuum tube to it to reflate her left lung. All this with this tiny baby, my Katie, just screaming. Just writing this note, I tear up, recalling that moment. I think it also is the main reason I have watched over her and always been a bit more protective of her, and continue to this day.

I do not recall the number of weeks she spent in the NICU, but I do recall the many days I would gown and glove, go into her room and reach my hand through the side port of the incubator to touch her and talk to her and watch her sleep. I also recall an event around the third day after her birth, being in the NICU with her, seeing Mary coming down the hall from outside the room (many windows) to make her first visit. I looked down for just a moment, and when I looked up, Mary was gone. Strange, I thought, but how difficult it was to see this tiny baby in the incubator with tubes in her chest; I put it out of my mind for that moment. Then suddenly, I saw a nurse run up to where she had been, then a second nurse, now with both bending over to attend to something or someone on the floor. I walked around the incubator, and looked down over the windowsill to see Mary passed out on the floor. I was going to help; however, within a few seconds, a large group had gathered to tend to her. The nurse in the NICU suggested I not go out at this time as the team was best able to attend to her needs. She was fine; she came again but did not attempt any further visits for a number of days.

Kate has grown up to be a wonderful young lady, more caring and compassionate than almost anyone I know. She has two young children of her own and presently works as a master's level Speech Pathologist. Both she and her children never cease to amaze me. As you probably remember from the above, both Bill and Maureen were very capable and did very well at avoiding trouble. Bill from not getting into much trouble and Maureen from her mastery of doing things that should get her in trouble and manipulating her way around that trouble. Kate, however, did neither. She would do things that would get her in trouble, and then she would get caught. She would attempt some daring maneuvers that her siblings had performed, but she would end up with a cut lip.

There are a number of events, but I will recall a few. One relates to her early teens and a one-time smoking trial. While attending the Vilas County Fair, she and several friends decided it would be cool to smoke. So, one of them produced a pack of cigarettes, passed them around, and lit them. Of course, sheriffs' deputies were in attendance as they patrolled the fairgrounds. When they came across her small group, except for Kate, they all dropped their cigarettes and were, of course, home free. Kate, not having that quick hide or devious nature, got caught and ended up with a ticket.

One other occasion with Kate was a time when I had taken Mary to the clinic. We had left the children home alone. They were old enough, and with Bill in charge, we anticipated no problems. The clinic we visited was attached to the local hospital. It was just a bit disturbing when I suddenly heard the ambulance go out on a run with sirens and lights. But I figured it can't be my children. Soon, about 10 minutes later, the ambulance returned, and simultaneously there was a page for me to report immediately to the Emergency Room. Well, that really is an attention-getter.

So, off we ran to the ER. There we found all three children, Bill, and Maureen, waiting and Kate in the ER room receiving treatment. It seems that all three had decided to play soccer in our basement. Kate, however, had attempted to move our piano with her head. In the contest between the piano and her head, the piano was the clear winner. It was just a gash, but head bleeds are usually pretty fierce, and hers would not stop, so the other two children called 911. Anyway, with a couple of stitches and some cleanup, she was fine, but I think all five of us had our share of scares for that day.

Keeping with my theme of lessons learned growing up on the farm, I come back to my earlier idea that at death, we do not float off into "heaven" or "hell." Rather, it is those things which we have done in our lives and those things we have created will continue on after we are gone. If the creation or result was good, then our lives are deemed good as we view "heaven." If they are bad or evil, we are deemed to have gone to hell. This is a bit like the "pay it forward concept," and my learning was that when you do things that are good or act in ways that are considered appropriate, the impact you have will continue in that same manner. I see my children as the ultimate example of this belief.

Their mother and I worked very hard to instill positive learning and positive emotional intelligence. We provided examples of living well. Our teachings supported a positive lifestyle. Each of our children has grown and accomplished considerable learnings as well as led a lifestyle that would be considered good and positive in our society. Two have continued in the tradition of healthcare careers, which would mark the third generation of this within our family trees. Our third, Bill, is not in healthcare, but he is exceedingly strong in his field of learning and maintains a very benevolent and positive lifestyle.

From my early days when I sat on the hill and watched the sunrise and marveled at the splendor of all that our world could offer, I built upon the concept that we are just on this planet for a very short time, and our impact has to be made quickly and affirmatively. We must take care of the planet, and all that touches it; it is so very important to our continued existence on it. It is my interpretation that religion and the many different religions can meld into all types of beliefs and support each other equally well. Religion can meld into my scientific beliefs and understanding of our universe and still support a religious aspect together with that. My children, then, are a large part of my afterlife and my eternity. They have the values which Mary and I have indoctrinated them with. We have educated them to go beyond what we have done in our lives and to also support that with their children. If our values and behaviors are what society accepts as good, then our eternal gift is our children, our grandchildren, and those things we have done in our lives, which continue to support and have a positive impact on others. That is how I view my eternal life.

Chapter 14: Boy Scouts

Most people have many experiences in their life, and to either a greater or lesser extent, they change that person in some way. One of my experiences was a period of time I spent as a Leader in the Boy Scouts of America. I will begin this with my son William (Bill), who joined Cub Scouts (the younger version of boy scouts) at about 8-9 years of age. He really enjoyed scouting and the many activities and challenges it presented.

Bill was always interested in the outdoors and liked the idea of being closer to nature and completing tasks usually meant to be challenging. As a Cub Scout, you do a lot of camping and also things like soapbox car races and other outdoor survival-type activities. Bill was always good at these things, and he progressed through the Cub Scouts quickly and into the regular Boy Scouts. There too, he progressed rapidly through the various levels and badges that a boy would earn. Within just a couple of years, he was looking at an Eagle Scout rank and a project to do for this level.

Being a good parent, you like to support your children and help them with those pursuits in life which they choose. I, therefore, entered into the world of scouting in a more formal manner. The leader of a scouting group is called a Scout Master. They receive special training in how scouts progress and in the many activities which they do. The Scout Master of Bill's pack was concerned that Bill was moving through the ranks too quickly. This would result that his advancement and soon achieving the highest rank possible. This would, in turn, cause him to then lose interest in his future scouting activities. To best support this process and work more closely with Bill, it was suggested that I become a scouting parent and a part of the leadership for the troop.

Now, this sounded like a great idea, and nothing in my mind caused me any concern about taking on this role. To properly become familiar with scouting, it was then suggested that I, together with a number of other gentlemen from the area who were involved with other programs, would take the Scout Master training course. This seemed legitimate and harmless in concept. So, I signed up and attended a three-day training course at Camp Tesomas in Rhinelander.

Now, the month was March. And March in northern Wisconsin is still winter. But the season is starting to temper just a bit toward Spring. I was not worried as I knew the Camp had really nice cabins with heat and sleeping bunks, so off I went with my sleeping bag and a couple of changes of clothes.

Friday morning started with introductions and kind of a get-to-know-everyone and then moved into lectures on scouting and its many components. This all was inside a cabin which was heated to around 75 degrees F.

As the lecture progressed, we went into the various activities that scouts do, most of which are out of doors, and of course, we then went outside. Now it is about 17 degrees F. So, you would work up a bit of sweat inside and then go outside, where the sweat could freeze onto your body. Yes, it was a large contrast.

And we repeated this over and over throughout the day and the next two days to come. Now as a new and learning scout leader, I learned quickly that I did not have anywhere near the proper level of clothing along to deal with this situation. But my hopes were high that when evening came, and we settled into the warm cabins and then into the nice bunks, all this would soon be forgotten.

Yup, "forget it" would be a good term. As dark approached and we were still outside, the trainer informed us to pair up with another person and "construct a tent." In the dark, all before our retiring to bed. WHAT? PUT UP A TENT IN THE DARK? Yup, I heard that correctly. So, it became one of the more amusing functions, watching a bunch of guys who, first off, knew very little about how to set up a tent and, secondly, to do so in the dark. We were told this should take about 5 minutes for the boys. And, about one hour later, we were finished. WOOOO, finally, this meant we could go inside, eat and warm up again. HUH, what do you mean we are going to cook outside, eat and then spend the night in the tent? Another affirmative, we would be cooking a meal on a campfire, which we still had to build, eat, and then spend the night in our tent.

I must confess, I do not remember the meal, no recollection whatsoever. I do recall getting my sleeping bag and tote bag with clothes and all and bringing them into the tent. So, I rolled out my sleeping bag and placed my pillow, the tote bag that is, at the head of the sleeping bag. With dinner complete and total darkness, the only thing to do was crawl into the sleeping bag and catch a long night's sleep.

This is the point where several of the above facts all come together. Rhinelander, winter, cold, tent, outside, cold, and the still frozen ground, oh and don't forget cold, all come together for the great scouting experience. I always wondered why my son took a stocking cap with him. And why most of the people present had a small, short-legged cot which they placed under the sleeping bag, which keeps you off the ground. The harshest of elements, the frozen ground; we were all sleeping on the frozen ground except those who knew to bring a cot.

Actually, I am wrong about that statement "sleeping"; I was wide awake and freezing on the frozen ground. I shivered, and I shook and tried many different things, but all I got was a good 9 hours of shivering and wondering how the hell I had decided to do this. No sleep.

It was a very long night, but morning finally did come. Fortunately, breakfast was not ours to make, and it was served back inside the cabin. Warmth. Thank you, God, is all that seemed to be in my mind. And then, we went through another day of training using the inside alternating with the outside method of torture.

Training, I mean. Another meal made over the fire and then back to the sleeping bag for my second night of sleep. Now, after a day and a half of training, together with a lack of sleep, I found that I was exhausted. But the cold started out the night, winning from allowing me to sleep. One of the more experienced leaders, I suspect out of pity, had given me a stocking cap and that was helping. I do not recall the time of night, but I finally was able to fall asleep. Having already spent one whole night and now part of this night without sleep, I think your body simply accepts the cold, and you do finally fall asleep.

Okay, I suspect you are thinking, so what? This is not very interesting. But then something much more interesting happens. I suspect because of the cold, the multiple shocks of hot to cold to my body, and the lack of sleep, my mind must have taken a stroll down an unusual path, and I started to dream.

Very vivid and seemingly real dreams. I was in the woods, yup, got that correct, and it was dark. That is still right on. And what was I dreaming about? I was chasing a wolf. Yes, a wolf, which I was chasing, and he was nasty. Now this is where I know this was a bit of a delusion, as my reaction to him was to growl and snarl at the wolf and attack it to scare him away.

And I knew, the louder I growled, the better my chance of scaring him away. So, I was going after that wolf with just about all the energy I had, snarling, growling, and making other guttural noises, and sure enough, after a few moments, I was able to drive this wolf away.

Now recall, thinking back to my earlier paragraph, we were paired with two people for each tent. Just after I had driven the wolf away, I woke up. I slowly realized I had been dreaming this whole ordeal to scare away a savage wolf. As I awoke, I also wondered if I had made any noises while dreaming, as I was growling and roaring in order to chase this wolf. I very quietly waited, and hearing no stir from my fellow camper, I was relieved to feel I had apparently not outwardly manifested my wolf chase. Until about 10 seconds when my tent partner softly stated, "Are you alright"? There was a pause as I was trying to think of what a proper response would be. So, with great thought and plan, I said, "Yes, I am fine." Profound response. Well, I guess he figured out I was still alive after that life-and-death fight, which he heard, and my "yes" confirmed all was now fine.

Along came Sunday morning and, fortunately the final half day of our training. I was recognized with the badge of a true Scout Master and proceeded to never do this again. Bill went on to a level of double silver palms Eagle Scout and, in several scout-related functions such as Order of the Arrow, also achieved the highest level of rank in those programs. This was a great program for him, and I will forever recommend for young men to participate in scouting. It provides them with skills and leadership that will benefit them all through life. Just remember to dress warmly.

By this point, you have come to expect how I relate this to my lessons in life which I learned on the farm as I grew up. This one is very simple: DON'T SLEEP ON THE GROUND. And dress warm if you are going to be outside in northern Wisconsin in any month except perhaps July. That lesson had been there for all my years on the farm, but it took Scouting to bring it home.

Chapter 15: Appliance Pickups

As readers may now begin to see, I was able to work almost all of my adult life and even part of my juvenile life. I also had an affinity for buying things and therefore needed money with which to do so. My first CEO or full administrative job was as the Administrator of Northwoods Living Care Center in Phelps, WI.

During my time working at Northwoods, I also belonged to the Lions Club for the Phelps area. While the club had several fund-raising projects, the main project was picking up freon-based appliances that were old and recycling the components of each appliance through a contract with Wisconsin Electric (WE). Our club, over the roughly 5 years they did this project, was able to raise about $125,000 for local needs. Over time and as the bank account grew, the club members became apathetic with these monies and voted to quit the project for future years.

Being ambitious, I, and a friend named Fred, decided to take on the project and run it ourselves. This may sound like work much beyond the capability of two persons. However, Fred and I (as the two youngest members of the club) were doing around 90% of all the work for the project anyway. Our territory, or area of responsibility, was northern Wisconsin and the central upper peninsula of Michigan. It was all part of the Wisconsin Electric territory at that time.

Patrons would contact WE and give their old appliances to the program and get a savings bond. As the local contractor, we would pick up these freon-based appliances, which included air conditioners, freezers, and refrigerators. We would gather these up into a large semi-trailer, and when we had a full load, we would ship them to south Milwaukee to be recycled.

Our remuneration included both a trip fee (money for the travel we did) and an appliance fee (so much per item) that we brought in and recycled to Milwaukee. The travel with the program was somewhat interesting. But it was more the trips, experiences, and the many interactions with people whom we interacted with that provided the greatest level of interest. Those experiences are memorable. I will share some of the more memorable experiences.

In the time when just Fred and I provided the service, we each went on separate runs in order to reclaim more appliances. We each had a large, enclosed trailer and could hold around 15 to 18 appliances per trip. For myself, I would hire persons who help me with the heavy lifting and movement of these appliances. Often, they were located in a basement or location where two strong persons were needed to move them.

There was a town in the UP that experienced a high rate of birth defects. While I am unsure of what caused this, I recall hearing a banjo playing the theme song from Deliverance as we drove through town. Much of the town even looked like the set of the movie Deliverance. One particular experience comes to mind from this area. We were scheduled to pick up a small refrigerator for an outside building on a farm.

Our process was to call and schedule each visit as we needed a signature for each appliance picked up. It was not infrequent, however, that the customer would simply leave the appliance outside and not be at home during our visit, and we would pick them up without signature. On this particular visit, I was with Terri, a Lions club member and a WE employee. We arrived at the farm, looked around, and found what had been described as the small building where we could get the appliance. The only problem, no appliance was sitting outside. We walked up to the only door visible and listened for a moment. Hearing a TV or radio which was playing, we figured we were at the correct location and proceeded to rap on the door.

We heard some rather strange guttural sounds, which seemed to be a person but no words. We rapped a second time, and the sounds repeated, but no one opened the door. In an assumed fashion, we simply opened the door, expecting to see someone and speak with them. Terri was in the lead, but both of us were able to see inside as we opened the door. This time the noise was much louder and was not muffled by the door.

There was a person there, but with no torso or body from the waist down, just arms and hands. He got off of a very low bed and began crawling towards us, using his arms and hands to propel himself in what would appear like a salamander crawl. And it was he who was making the low and loud guttural sounds. Well, this is one of those moments, kind of like a science fiction movie, where the alien jumps out and eats you or at least maims you as he attacks. Both Terri and I made a similar soundless scream and shut the door, and jumped back away from the door. We could hear the person inside, but it was obvious he could not open the door. With the words, "Let's get the fuck out of here," we were back in the truck and speeding away. As time passed, Terri came to call the person the salamander man. For me, I just kind of put the memory away and suppressed it, as a good counselor would say.

Several months later, a repeat request to remove the appliance came, and we spoke with the family to learn that the person in the small house was named Ray. He was born with severe birth defects and was never able to attend school or function in society due to birth defects. His family made this small house where he lived for a number of years with the farm family support. We did ultimately pick up the appliance, but this time, it had been placed outside the building.

While the previous experience was probably our biggest surprise in doing these pickups, I do remember the best surprise I pulled off on one of my helpers. During the time I worked on the project for myself, I would hire a young gentleman whose father I worked with at the hospital. His name was John. He was young, energetic, and, as a high school male, full of raging hormones. As the story goes, on this particular trip, I would pick him up at his house, and then we would drive to the most distant pick-up to start our load. This was done to minimize our loaded mileage on the vehicle. We often left at 6:00 am in order to

cab of the truck, we both realized we needed to do something with it as it was illegal. We were completely unsure how to handle this illegal substance and did not want to be arrested with it in possession. After nearly a half hour of pondering what to do, I called a friend who served in law enforcement. He laughed and said, just empty it out the window. Wow, such a simple solution, yet so hard to think of that as we pondered more about the illegality of this item. I think people get so caught up in one aspect of a situation that they completely forget to think about any other aspect.

Well, I end this chapter with the note that these experiences probably would be in question as to my farm theme. But with my farm theme, I note that I acquired the ability to do a great deal of work and do so without regard to a clock or time. I learned what I call critical thinking skills and the ability to make a plan on how to best accomplish a series of tasks in a given time period. It supported learning ways in which to accomplish work when at times a job seemed impossible. And taking all these things together, it gave me a mastery of managing organizations which I have used all of my life. Lastly, during the two years I performed this project for myself, it provided me with around $55,000 in income and allowed me to pay off the loan on my home in under three years. My years on the farm taught me all these valuable learnings and abilities.

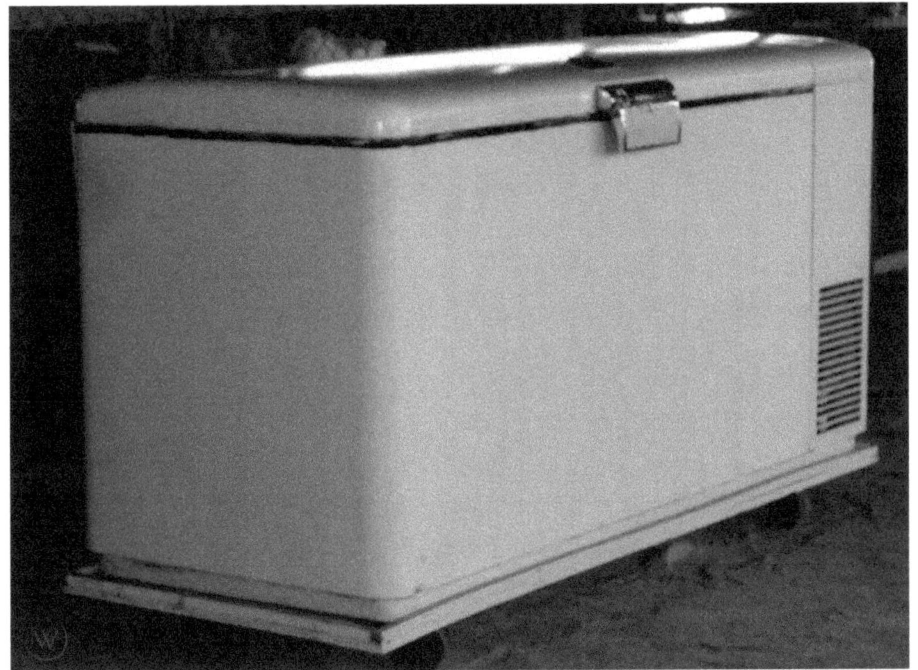

Chapter 16: My One Big Trip

As I was reflecting on my life, I pondered how I would describe some of the more recent. While I cannot call him an event per se, Mike is certainly an interesting person worthy of a chapter because of the many adventures we have experienced together and a few that he has experienced alone. Mike would count among the several persons I have considered my close friends. By background, he was a Physician Assistant-Certified or PAC for short. This is a medical person, somewhat like a physician but with fewer years of college and on-the-job training. I met Mike as the Administrator of Northwoods Living Care Center (NLC) in Phelps. This would make our years of acquaintance about 25 at the time of this writing.

Mike grew up in northern Wisconsin and had spent most of his life in the northern areas. At the beginning of our work together, we lived around the Eagle River and Phelps area. My initial meeting was to recruit and hire him to practice medicine in the hospital's Emergency Room Services in Phelps. Given the very small size of the NLC facility, it also meant that we would associate outside of the roles we played within the hospital and work setting. Mike owned numerous low-cost houses and therefore was also a landlord in the north woods area. Our first real connection, which occurred outside of work, was when he was needed to cover the emergency room. A house he was desirous of owning was being sold at a sheriff's sale. He talked me into going to the auction, registering, and bidding on the house he desired to purchase. I do not recall all the logistics of this time, but I actually went to the Courthouse and bought the house on his behalf. I successfully accomplished what he had set out to do with this purchase. This then made us not only work associates but friends for future times.

I forget the year but one of our most interesting times was the decision we made to take a two-week trip and travel together to Texas, then to the Grand Canyon, and finally to the Dakotas for a tour of the Southwest USA. The trip, however, was planned to make the experience more unique than what most people would consider a normal trip. To begin, I purchased a full-sized Chevrolet conversion van that had about 200,000 miles on it. This was to be our travel vehicle. Together, we established a lodging rule that we would only stay in motels where we could secure (and often bargain for) a room under $30 per night for both of us together. This was a time when a cheap motel was about $50-$60 per night, and a nice one was about $90. So, this became the main challenge of the trip. If we did not find such a room, we would then default to sleeping in the van. The van was a conversion van, so sleeping in it was a viable option. The van, however, being old and having curtains and other amenities, also looked similar to those that persons use to kidnap children. My loving family, therefore, coined it "The Abduction Van." On one occasion, I was driving down the road, and they happened to be in a different car but on the same road. They passed me and held up a large sign which read, "let those children go". Yeah, really funny.

Now, if the above were not complicated enough of a trip with this old van, I had recently sold a replica Ford Cobra car to a person in Plano, Texas. I had decided this would be a perfect way to deliver the car and collect my $17,000 in cash. So, I rented a U-Haul car carrier and loaded the car onto it, and attached this trailer and all behind the van. And the next morning, we began our adventure.

After our first day on the road, we ended up in Oklahoma City, Oklahoma. We went in search of some place to buy diner, and for a short while, I had Mike drive the van, being a bit tired after much driving. Somewhere we became a bit lost, and in our search, we ended up on some side streets. Recall the trailer we were pulling. To get back to more traveled roads, we had to maneuver around in a parking lot. Without regard for the trailer nor the age of my van, Mike made a sharp turn to the left and literally pulled the tie rod end out of the main tie rod housing. Now, driving meant our front right tire going right and our front left tire going left, we were suddenly going nowhere. Vehicles do not easily go two different directions at one time.

Now, back to the learnings from the farm, I had learned that you always carry a good set of tools with you. Especially if you are driving an old van. So, I crawled underneath the front of the van, saw the problem, and by turning the steering wheel slowly and in unison with the tires going in the same direction, I was able to push the tie rod end back into the main tie rod receiver, tighten this connection, and once again have my front tires aiming in somewhat the same direction. The only problem was I had no way to align the tires so that we could drive the many miles left on our trip. We knew that the audible sound of a tire squealing as we drove was not a good sign.

So, we began our hunt for a car parts store. By now, it was 5:00 pm on a weekday, and most were all closed. Now luck is always a wonderful friend, and I think he was our third passenger for much of this trip. We came to an auto parts store which was closed, but the managers were still closing out the cash register. By pounding on the window of an auto parts store, we were able to get the attention of a manager. And again, luck jumped in, and he came to the door to help us. He was able to find the part we needed, had one, and with the proper amount of cash in hand, we now had the part we needed.

To keep on time with our travel plans, we needed to get the part installed that night, not take your chances on the next day. The car parts person suggested there were three Vietnamese persons who worked in a private garage nearby. They liked nights since it was cooler in which to work. We drove slowly there and miraculously found them and their garage. Despite some English challenges, we were able to convince them to install the part we had just purchased.

We unhooked the trailer and my Cobra car and drove the van into the garage with the tire still squealing. Within about an hour and a half, the part was installed. But a fast visual inspection was able to diagnose that the left tire faced a bit left and the right a bit right. So now the question became how do you align a tire without one of the modern alignment machines?

Something new to me was a process were you take a sting from the back tire to the front and hold it tight; you have the string touch both the front and back of the front tire at the same time. This results that the front tire is in alignment with the back tire. Then going to the other side, you do the same, bringing the string from the back tire to the front tire. The only difference is you adjust the alignment of that tire not by steering it but by the tie rod adjuster until it also touches the front and back of the tire at the same time. By doing so, both tires are now parallel and able to drive down the road as normal, and you are ready for the road.

It was a bit past midnight, but we were ready for the road and our first $29 motel. Day one is done.

The next day, we arrived in Plano, TX, and I found my buyer for the Cobra. After a bit of back and forth, we learned that a replica car does not have its serial number on the vehicle. We had to find a punch set and actually pound a serial number into the frame of the car before the buyer would finish the purchase.

But after a bit more time on the ground, under the vehicle, it was done, my car now had a serial number that matched the title, and I was now carrying $17,000 in cash. We dropped the trailer at a U-Haul drop site and were off to Austin to see my son.

The remainder of our stay in Austin was a lot of fun, taking in the capital, the Alamo, and several missions. The only somewhat cumbersome event was parking on a steep hill at my son's apartment. I had a very low fuel amount in the van, and finding that the uphill park could leave the fuel uptake no longer in the fuel, my fuel was officially empty. So, with a gas can in hand, we added about 5 gallons of gas and were again on the road.

Our next stop was Carlsbad Cavern. The Cavern was extraordinary. And from there, we next went to the Grand Canyon.

Now, I do not recall if I mentioned this, but one of my biggest fears was a fear of heights. Anything above the second rung on a ladder was too high for me. For those of you who know the Grand Canyon, I recall there are cliffs from which you can fall and not hit the ground again for a minute or more. And that is a long way down. And all this with a new tie rod end on the van with 200,000 miles and a string alignment. I do not recall the amount of time, but I know there were many moments wondering how Mike had ever talked me into taking this old van to the Grand Canyon for our "adventure." But we made it to the top and started our tours and views.

Back to Mike. Mike, unlike me, had no fears of heights. So, as we started our first trail walk, he was about a foot from the edge and me about 20 feet away. So, he decided to have some fun with me. He pretended to walk very near the edge, slip, and look as if he was going to fall over the edge. Holly cow, this scared the crap out of me (farm term), another "Oh shit" moment. But even more funny, there was a lady who happened to be watching him from a different direction. I think she fainted or at least went down on a bench and was not able to stand for several moments. She had screamed as he neared the edge and must have absolutely believed she was witnessing a death. Seeing her, he quickly got up, and we did hurry to distance ourselves from her.

The rest of this part of the adventure was simply breathtaking, and I was even able to get a bit closer to the cliffs after a while. This is a sight that everyone in their lifetime must see.

We did spend one night in the van while traveling to the opposite side of the Canyon. It was a bit cold at night, but as soon as the sun rose, we almost got cooked out. The metal on the side of van actually clicked from the heat. This was our first night in the van sleeping.

The next leg of our adventure took us into Arizona and the desert. Once again, as Mike was driving, our disaster number 2 occurred. Mike had the habit of flooring the gas pedal going up hills to not slow down. I quickly found that in the hot desert, this is not what you want to do with an old, tiring transmission. And, of course, he blew the transmission out. Only reverse and second gear are are left. We were able to travel for a short distance but only at a slow rate. We pulled the van into a road crew work area just off the highway and parked.

And one more time, our third passenger, Mr. Luck, came along, and we were able to get a ride from one of the road workers from the site we had parked at. She was a nice Indian lady who was going back to her home in a little town. Mike road with her while I stayed with the van. Fortunately, we were able to get a large towing flatbed truck to retrieve the van and haul it back to his repair station. He was located in Stamford, AZ. I will never forget the town. And as luck would have it, he worked on transmissions.

We spent the night at a cheap motel in Stamford, and the next morning, we spent calling my son and using my phone to search for a rebuilt transmission. Did I mention luck? Once again, we were able to find a rebuilt transmission of perfect fit and whatever else the van needed. It seems that the largest rebuilder of old transmissions in the USA is located in Arizona.

We rented a vehicle and drove to Phoenix, AZ, where we were able to pick up the transmission. We even got to enjoy our travel through the desert and, within the same day, get back to have the transmission to the repair shop. Thank you again, Mr. Luck.

The time we arrived back at the repair station was late afternoon, and the repair person simply did not want to start pulling and replacing a transmission at that time. Drawing on my lessons from the farm, I had learned that busy people do not like to be interrupted. So, speaking with the shop owner, I suggested it was not a problem for him to install the next day; we would simply sit around and talk with him as he worked.

Now, I might be offended that he did not entertain my company as worth his while, but he actually worked through the entire night, and when we returned the next morning, the van was off the rack and ready to drive. I guess he did not want the pleasure of my company. In short, blowing the transmission and securing a new one and having it installed had cost us only one added day in our adventure.

These were the fun times and best memories of the times with Mike. Now comes the lesser times. Mike, in the years which followed, transitioned into more of a hoarder. He is a hoarder of low cost, often in bankruptcy houses, and a hoarder of junk which he calls treasure. I have been able to watch the TV series called Hoarders, and I think Mike has them all beat. He has more houses hoarder full and probably more "stuff" of mixed nature than any of the hoarders in these shows. For the sake of sticking to the theme of this writing, I will not go into much detail, but the one thing the farm taught me is you do not need junk. It only piles up, and someday someone must clean it up. My lesson from the farm and my dad was when you hoard "stuff" later in life, it has to be cleaned up. I have tried to impart this knowledge to Mike, and I have failed. Where is Mr. Luck when I need him now?

Chapter 17 : Mike

Since I have introduced you to Mike, I will detail my relationship with him. This chapter will deal with Mike and some of his more unusual attributes. To start the tone of this chapter, as long as I have known Mike, he has always introduced me as the "richest man he knows."

This is not true, but I do know that I could surely introduce him as the "cheapest man I know." On *People Search*, his total assets are listed as slightly over $2 million, so he may well be the richest man I know.

The TV series "Hoarders" shows persons that have hoarded a house and sometimes a property full of their hoarded goods. Generally, the hoard consists of junk and sometimes even what is more properly termed trash. Mike is a hoarder. He not only hoards what I will refer to as stuff, but he accumulates numerous housing properties and has even lived in several of them. He has literally hoarded five of them full of stuff, together with the garages and even the land which goes with them. To define his stuff, which by the way he calls treasures, let me share a few examples. These would include plastic dolls with the head and arms broken off, broken bungy cords, tools that have rusted beyond any use, and even multiple old vehicles that do not run. It would pretty much include almost anything you can think of that regular people would dispose of. As I mentioned, he calls them treasures. I have spoken to him on this subject on numerous occasions, and he further defines his reason for keeping all these items is based upon his claim that "you never know when you might need something from this stash." One of these examples he spoke of is the broken baby buggy with only two wheels left on it. He tells me there are usable parts there, and you never know when you might need some piece of this. Now to clarify a bit further, Mike is 74 at the time of this writing, and in my opinion, the chances of ever needing a baby buggy again to repair something in his life is very remote.

As mentioned above, Mike has lived in about 5 of these houses. In all cases, between the house and garages, and other outbuildings, he has completely hoarded these structures fully, literally up into the rafters. In a couple of instances, he does have in these buildings items that are actually usable, functional items, such as his skid steer, which is stored in the garage at his Phelps house. But for the rest of the garage, there are bags full of empty soda cans, old doors from torn down buildings, old tires, stair steps torn out from a house, and much, much more. The garage is literally full into the rafters, and it is a three-car garage.

The is a second two-car garage on this property with many items stored in it also. The outside of both the house and the two garages are circled with many items. These things surround the perimeter of each building by about a 20 to 50-foot span. Included with these items are about 6 vehicles that do not run and have not been used for 20-plus years. They have sat so long that the tires are literally now sunk into the ground by about 10 inches.

I recall the green Chevy pickup truck that we tried to move about three years ago. Even with my 4-wheel drive vehicle hooked onto it, I was unable to even move it a slight bit. Worse yet, all 4 tires had gone flat, so we had to start by airing them up. We quickly found that the aluminum wheels where now unable to hold air sufficient to move the vehicle. We then used a large floor jack to lift the truck, and with a number of wood and cement blocks, we attempted to block it up in order to get the wheels off for repair of the tires. Several hours later, we had the front two tires up but were unable to lift the rear.

To end this part of the story, it is now a year later, and the vehicle still sits there with two wheels up and two probably more sunken into the earth. I should have mentioned that there was a skid steer in the garage but it had been driven into the the garage so that access to the battery panel could not be made, and after sitting for many years, the battery was dead. So, no functional skid steer.

I move on to his home nearest me, the Eagle River home. This is actually a house, together with a smaller cabin and a two-car garage. The garage is filled into the rafters with old shingles and miscellaneous building materials, most of which are well-used and have been saved from other building tear-downs and stored.

The cabin is interesting as it would be a neat item were it not filled with the items from Mike's deceased parents, together with more stuff Mike has decided to save. It would normally be a two-bedroom, one-bath building but other than a narrow walkway to get into one bedroom, it is filled to the ceiling with "stuff". It was broken into several years ago, and nothing ended up being stolen. Imagine that poor robbers are finding all these treasures.

Now move onto the house. The house has its own interesting story. Many years ago, after Mike had moved out of this house, he rented it to a single gentleman. That man was unable to pay his power bill but had a number of car batteries in the basement and a diesel semi-truck he drove for his job. He would bring the truck to the house, hook up the battery from the truck, run the engine all night and charge up his batteries. Based on the remains from when the house burned down, it was also very certain he was producing Meth in the basement.

I mentioned the house burning down. Well, Mike had just given him an eviction notice for unpaid rent, and wonder of wonders, on one of the coldest nights in winter, with a high wind blowing, the house caught fire, and all was lost. Well, except for all the tools and things the renter had just moved out the night before. Now you might think this gave Mike legal action against this man, but not so, as he was a member of a notorious biker gang, and he threatened Mike's life on several occasions.

Mike went into what he described as bad depression. I suspect this in part due to the fact that he does not carry insurance on any of his properties. It would take him about five years to accept this and start to rebuild the house. I should also mention he has the power turned off at all properties that he does not live in, so even when he goes to one to work on it, he needs many warm blankets.

The burned house on this property was a two-bedroom house with a full basement. After the fire, the cement portion of the basement was still present and intact. The wood portion was a pile of rubbish. It had to be rebuilt. So, with many weeks and months of my help, Mike managed to get the prior burned structure removed and a new house started. I did spend time on the rebuild, helping put up walls, drywall, and other components. Sadly now, probably 15 years later, it sits there with partial drywall, and you guessed it, it is full of treasure.

Now, an even more interesting part of this story goes to the fact that Mike's hoarding problem, in almost all cases, moves outside the building walls once the inside is filled. This property is no different was already surrounded by "stuff," including four unusable boats, two wrecked pontoon boats, and piles of burnt lumber he had pulled from the previous house. The old boats that were not seaworthy and many other items from his rentals included an old countertop system, some old lake buoys, and many more piles of other old junk, which generally came when a renter moved out and did not take these things with them.

The next-door neighbor, who was not a good neighbor but had built a very large and fashionable house, loved to show off their house and yard. The Misses loved her clean yard so much that even a leaf falling from the trees commanded an immediate fire up of the leaf blower and getting the leaf away. And, of course, they hated Mike. Imagine a pristine view in three directions and a "dump" in the remaining one. Also, imagine the entire boarder of these two properties lined with junk.

The feud between them had started many years before and, after an expensive lawsuit, had really created a level of hatred not before seen in this area. So, as Mike added to his hoard, the tensions only continued to grow. And finally, a call went to the zoning Commissioner and the County Health Department to attempt to get it moved or destroyed in some fashion. And, of course, Mike responded by adding more stuff. The straw that broke the camel's back was an old shed that was ready to fall down and a bright orange fence was was placed to denote the property line.

I recall this fight going on for about two years. Finally, after the county's threat of fine and forfeiture, Mike did remove much of his stuff but merely relocated it to other houses he owned. Some also were moved under the deck of the house being built, and a large tarp was placed over the deck of the house to hide the stuff under that tarp.

There are many stories, and I could write another book based on an accumulation of these stories. But I will end this chapter and discuss Mike's most recent home in Wausau. I end here because it may be the greatest of all disbelief I will leave you with.

I estimate about 13 years ago; Mike purchased a very small 2-bedroom house in Wausau. This was done to be near his mother, who was getting very aged and needed help. About four years after he moved there, she became frail enough to justify moving in with Mike. She was a small and very nice little lady who passed away about four years ago.

But, back to the house. Of course, the purchase of this house was like all others, as the house was in bankruptcy and needed considerable attention. And this made it very cheap. Mike's perfect house. Cheap.

As he moves in, he finds that the well does not meet the code and must be replaced. This becomes a part of the transaction with the bank, and a new well is drilled on the property. After several months a well water test is required only to find that it is contaminated with lead and about three other lethal chemicals.

It was very near an old gas station that had moved many years earlier but left the ground contaminated. After a long fight ensued with the bank who he purchased the house from, they agreed to drill one more well with a cap on the total costs. This well was approximately over 300 feet and was even fracked to make it produce ample water supply. The result was even worse in this well in that it will only produce about 2-3 gallons of water before it has to recover and will only produce after a period of time goes by. And it has even more contaminants than the previous well and at higher levels.

So now Mike is faced with no water, only a well sufficient to provide water for a toilet flush. There was city water and sewer available, but the cost to install was around $25,000. Now for most people, this would be a problem, but for my pal Mike, not at all. He sets up large plastic barrels under the eaves troughs of the garage and house and has fresh rainwater to wash in.

He next takes out a membership at the YMCA. When he attends, this gives him a chance to bathe. And drinking water can be secured almost anywhere simply by taking a number of used milk jugs and refilling them, and using this water for consumption. The "Y" also serves that purpose. But then comes winter, and the wash water becomes ice. So, Mike being the industrious and frugal person he is, buys bundles of clothes at year-end thrift shop sales and wears clothes for a couple of weeks, then throws them out. Wow, all the needs are answered in one place. Wash water, drinking water, and bathing are all paid for by Medicare as they cover the cost of a gym membership. And toss your clothing when it gets soiled, and life could not be much less expensive. If you do this properly, you can even put some clothes into the shower, and they are washed while you wear them. I come back to my opening premise, is this the cheapest man you know or what?

As I was watching a session of the show <u>Hoarders</u> this past week, it was eerie how close these persons resemble Mike. It was also interesting to note that the typical traits of hoarders include intelligence, compassion, conservativism, and kindness. And while he is strange, he very much does possess these positive qualities. I often wonder, when he passes away, who is going to clean up all this "stuff" or treasure, as he calls it.

Now you will also recall the thesis of my book centers around the idea of things I learned growing up on a farm and how they impacted my later life. My father was a bit of a hoarder. He had buckets and buckets of old bolts and small parts that he would buy at farm auctions that occurred around our home. Similarly, you recall our use of older farm equipment and the often-needed repair before we could go into the field and perform the needed work. This meant then having several of the same types of equipment as a backup for others broken down and needing repair. That could be described as being a bit of a hoarder.

When my father passed away, and it came time to clean up the farm, we had days and days of throwing stuff away. Much of this, we wondered why he would have purchased it and, secondly, why he would have kept it all. The many pails of rusty bolts and nails we ended up hauling to the recycling center and barrels of used drain oil. No value but many pounds of iron and gallons of old oil. My learning was that hoarding is not a good thing and using old machinery which has outlived its life will be very inefficient. In the long run, it is best not to possess large excesses of "stuff" and have the correct tool for the job, one that functions properly.

I have had to "clean up" several estates, and while the original owner may have felt there was some reason to save things of little need and no value, it simply never is a positive thing. There is hardly ever a time when the hoard has something you need, and even when it does, you often need help finding it. It ties up resources, and as our nation experiences the impacts of the greenhouse effect, it only makes more and more good sense to recycle all that you can.

The many dumps which now exist, the huge amounts of carbon we have put back into the atmosphere, and the destruction of earth and land all have come to create problems with our planet. These seem only to be getting worse and doing so more rapidly. So, the lesson is don't hoard; recycle all you can. Don't store away what you don't need. And lastly, be respectful of the planet and keep it as close to what it is when a man is not present. In this somewhat strange sort of way, this ties together with many of the other thoughts and values I have learned.

Chapter 18: 2020

2020 is an interesting number. It has always stood for perfect vision when a vision test is conducted. The year 2020, however, was far from an ideal year. I think the events of the year 2020 warrant a bit of review relative to my philosophies. While I am sure our society and political analysts will massively overanalyze this time period, I will throw my hat into this ring and add to the analysis.

The beginning of the year was like most others; of course, living in Wisconsin meant lots of snow and cold, and the 2019/2020 winter was not an exception. As the year started, very early, we heard of a new virus, a coronavirus and that was first found in China. People thought most likely it reached humans in their open food markets. When you would see pictures, it appears that virtually any type of animal was considered edible in China. The early theories centered around the transference of the virus from animals to humans. I am a picky eater, so this seemed crude and certainly not within my comfort zone.

And then came the barrage of news reports and much conflicting information about the virus. Being in the healthcare field all my life, I have learned that there are disease-causing entities that can be very nasty. Nasty, meaning they can result in your death or severe harm to your body. Because my career, at the time of this writing, was involved with Nursing Homes and Skilled Nursing Care facilities, the early news was about 20 deaths in a Washington state nursing home. This was an extreme alert for me. Very fortunately, the home I work with took immediate steps to mitigate the impact of this virus, and the impact was minor. In the late spread process, we did have some staff infect some clients, but overall, our nearly 300 clients were kept safe.

Next, I want to review the actions and many events that ended up relating to our government leader, President Trump. As I have noted in earlier chapters, I view our purpose on the planet to not only look out for ourselves but to be a positive force in society and leave a legacy that betters our planet and the life on it. As a species, we function not only for our own self-needs, but we function to support, protect, and be a viable part of the whole of all species. Our more often used term is society when it comes to man. My view and its role in things like a pandemic come through the things I have done throughout my life, which will continue after me. I view this through my ideals of what religion means for me, and I view this through my children and the others whose lives I have impacted over time.

Lastly, I view this through continuously asking myself if what I am doing will have a positive and a lasting impact on our planet and life on that planet. Recall this is my understanding of what the prime purpose of being a farmer was and is.

Now, I shift to Donald J. Trump. If there could be a polar opposite of what I believe in, it would be Donald J. Trump. Everything he does is without regard for our planet. He acts only upon his personal wants regardless of any benefit for the future, regardless of society, or regardless of anyone within society. He acts solely for his own benefit and wants.

I want to share my observations and thoughts on this and contrast them with my values. The ability to grow produce on a farm and the actions which take place which cause them to grow are all based on various forms of science. This science includes biology, chemistry, and physics. I think my ability to understand various scientific teachings and, similarly, my mathematical background has formed how I view the world. The way all these things respond in nature is very logical and predictable. We collectively call this "Mother Nature," the environment, and other names, but it all responds to biological, physical, and chemical-based processes and rules. Everything follows a very strict and knowable pattern. As a farmer, there are many ways to acquire this knowledge. Some of this is just observed and learned by rote memory. The deeper understandings and study show that it is based upon many forms of scientific fact. And like all living things, they have one main goal, and that is to continue to exist and do so by replication. This ongoing life, together with the reproduction process, then becomes the key to how you manage the continuation of any living entity.

Back to Covid. A virus lives and replicates within its host. Early in the COVID pandemic, a decision was made to pretend it was going away shortly. This premise causes very little fear among people and is foolish at its very best. And further, to focus on political matters, during this same time, we ignored the process of the virus and its spread and impact on society. Our MAGA leader did this to simply appear stronger and present a more popular impression of his ability.

We know from many different germs and viruses that they are very good at what they do when it comes to reproduction. The process to shut them down is to interrupt what we need to do to stop them from spreading and reproducing. This includes masking, social distancing, hand washing, and providing a way to keep people from coming in close contact with one another.

But our President was focused on money. Recall that his alleged empire was mostly motels and resorts, all of which depended on a robust economy and a population that travels and uses alternative overnight sleeping quarters. This also results in frequent social contact. This would be the opposite of what actions are needed to stop or slow a pandemic. Sadly, economic impacts equal business and make money, so ignore all these science-based facts and keep that business rolling along. This is where our nation's leaders show their true goals. Do we save lives, or do we make more money? The farm has taught me we can do both but must produce serious plans to accomplish these seemingly conflicting goals. You educate people, you temper business but not cut it off, and you put your knowledge to work on the best ways to avoid spreading the virus.

Next, let's go on and look at even more of the Trump presidency. Yes, the reader will certainly know I am an anti-Trumper. Not so much the person, rather, I believe his selfish goals directed his actions, and he lives for the moment, not the future. His values are selfish, and his respect for the future of our world is nil. It is these qualities with which I disagree.

First is global warming, or the impact which the species…man has on the planet, mostly by the production of great amounts of carbon. As a farmer, one of the first lessons you learn is of the great ability of our planet, our land, our earth to heal itself. Based on science, things attempt, when left to their own volition, will return to normal or seek the most stable state possible. Our planet is wonderful at taking things that affect it and healing or returning itself to its most stable state. Rain replenishes the moisture in soil, lighting replenishes the ozone, plants offset and use the carbon dioxide and carbon monoxide created by animals and man and return them as oxygen. The erosion of rock and minerals creates soil, and the list goes on literally forever. Even the species of man, which has overtaken much of the planet with building structures, roads, and vehicles burning carbon-based fuels, can be managed by our planet's healing processes. There is, however, a limit to what can happen as a normal continuing process of healing. When something occurs that overpowers these healing processes, the processes themselves intensify to bring the planet back to its most balanced status. The amount of carbon in the air increases the retention of solar heating and creates a greenhouse effect. This, in turn, melts the polar ice caps on the planet's north and south poles. This, in turn, releases more water into the liquid form, which puts more water into the atmosphere. With this chain effect, more heat and more liquid (water) together cause more moisture to exist in the atmosphere. This, in turn, creates more rain, more violent storms, more and bigger tornados, and much larger hurricanes. All this is simply the earth healing itself and attempting to return to balance. But again, Mr. Trump simply says, I need bigger donations from the oil and coal business, so we frack the earth and burn more oil and coal. Just so he gets bigger political donations. And our planet responds with greater floods, more destruction from tornados, hurricanes, and other weather-related events. Our great planet simply keeps healing itself, and as needed, it intensifies this whole process. Sadly, Donald simply only thinks of his personal wants and never those of society or the world.

Next, I will share my thoughts relative to Mr. Trump's tending of his flock. As President, it is my expectation and the expectation of our founding fathers that once elected, the President serves **all of America.** My farm life taught me that there are big and small animals present on farms. Some need a lot of care, and some are very independent in their needs. They are together with a mix of stronger and weaker animals, but they all live together with no one dominant over the other. Each has all their basic needs being met. This would include shelter, food, water, and whatever care they would need.

While the stated Constitution of our country and events, such as the Civil War, was waged with the goal of making all people equal, our nation, for the majority of our existence, needs to do better with this premise. We have failed in many ways. The farmer knows he must care for all his animals and crops with equal quality and diligence, or when harvest time comes, he will face shortfalls and starvation. Our nation has moved toward making some things more equal, but the prejudices and politics of our many cultures continue to exist. To me, Mr. Trump personifies these differences and inequalities. He does this through the use of social media and a clever way of wordsmithing his ideals. This results in inciting people to follow him and giving him great amounts of funding and blind trust in following his words. And as always, rather than look at the best for the flock, he looked at how he could gain personally from this. Just as Mussolini and Hitler did during their reign, he incited many people through the hate and prejudice of others. Through lying and rhetoric, he was able to draw a large following. Through racial bias and inequality, he was able to use the racial discrimination which exists in our nation, prey upon the feelings of the blue-collar middle class who have lost many jobs in America, and he convinced them these jobs were stolen by other countries, by minorities, by immigrants and by anyone else they chose to hate. The reality of America since World War II was that most of these jobs were eliminated by automation and robotics. Robots are more dependable, less costly, and more accurate in their task performance compared to people in many of these historical jobs.

An example of this I learned of recently was that our nation produces about 80 million cars per year. This was true 20 years ago and is true today. The only difference is that we now do so with about 5% of the original workforce doing this production. Sadly, today's cars are far more efficient, last many times longer and perform better, and have higher quality than in the past. Mr. Trump led his followers to believe by attacking foreigners, immigrants, and other nations; this would all reverse. And now, four years later, these people are even more angry. If the farmer used this thought, he might have one large bull and no other animals on his farm. While that bull would certainly be dominant beyond all compare, that farmer will not survive. Mr. Trump may go work on a farm for some period of time.

Continuing, Mr. Trump used racial discord and bias and placed his focus on white Christians to build his support. Historically that is the dominant race and religious makeup of our country. As I stated above, these persons are mostly made up of the blue-collar working persons. Unchanged for the last 100 years and much of the history of our country, we have suffered from a deep and continuous racial bias. He carefully played on this bias and built what could be called a cult of people who supported and followed him. While this is not all of America, these people view themselves as superior to other races. They see Trump as almost a savior of the country as his promise was to make America great again, meaning let's return to the past when white was dominant. The white middle-class Christian controlled America for decades, even centuries.

As I have done throughout this writing, I turn to the farm and science. The species of man is one species, not dozens like we racially divide. Through hereditary impacts, we may have different skin colors and body structures, but when we look at DNA, we are one and the same. It is only our upbringing that has given us bias and prejudices which we have. Sadly, the fomenting and agitation of certain beliefs cause the strife we now see acutely within our nation. Using my farm learnings, they are not real they are merely beliefs that we act upon. Just imagine if the farm animals all decided they were each supreme and should destroy the other different animals to secure dominance. It would be crazy.

In my closing thoughts of the four years ending in 2020, we all know Donny's 30,000 lies were a clear winner if lying were the goal. But leading with lies does little else other than divide and anger people. Creating fear and hatred only incites people. Having a bully as a leader takes us nowhere. He does not lead by great wisdom, passion, or promise. He does not lead by great accomplishments; he does not inspire people to greatness; he simply was the biggest bull in the pen. Again, let's look at the farm. A strong flock of 100 chickens will be able to produce nearly 100 eggs a day when the flock is maintained well. But enter a dominant chicken who only looks for themselves, not the flock, and the rest suffers. You lose much of the flock, and many within the flock become weak, and this gives the dominant chicken even more strength. You sacrifice many and most of the flock to support dominance and provide for the needs of only a few. Soon all others are weak and unable to produce. So now you gather only a small number of eggs each day. So, while the one flourishes and can brag about what they can do, the remainder of the flock dies or languishes, and the farmer loses. The bully always has to win; there can be no other, not ever. But the farmer with only a few eggs or only a couple of the prize cows will soon be out of business.

Ah, yes, the farm is a great teacher. Many other things in our life teach us and would have a great impact on our life if we would allow them to happen, learn from them, or better yet, seek these lessons that can be learned as they appear all around us. 2020 should be a great teacher. But I see a few people that learn. There may be more to come; it will be most interesting to see what we learn when 2020 is reviewed historically and how we respond to it. The simplicity of the farm and its lessons can teach us how to be better people. Oh, my departing thought goes back to the bull; the farm taught me never to follow the bull as he roams about; you will only get one thing on your shoes.

Epilogue

When I decided to attempt to write a book, I began by thinking about what was meaningful in my life. Writing the book made me think even more about the events of my life, what I learned from them, and how the early events shaped the later events. There were always ongoing relationships if you looked for them. While my first years of life were a bit boring, they formed a base for me upon which subsequent events grew and developed. They were never individual isolated events by themselves. Still, rather a flow of continuous actions that each impacted on the next and in some way formed and contributed to later events. They were my best teachers in life.

My years on the farm taught me humility; they made me strong in physical stature and mental agility. Above all, they helped me to develop my sense of right and wrong and to give me a road map for my entire life. I recall an old saying, "If you don't know where you are going, any road map will get you there." a farmer and all the things the farm allowed me to do gave me a destination for my life and guidance on how to do this best. My early days on the farm gave me an appreciation of life on our planet, and when I combined this with my education, this came together to fit into a complex yet complete picture1

of what life is. I jokingly asked what the meaning of life is, and in hindsight, the farm answered that question.

I can look beyond just the culture I was part of and see how other cultures fit equally well into my concepts. I see how all religions could be correct and fit together with science and physics in our known world. I saw how the evolution of our species could occur as scientifically, it has been proven and still accommodate all religious facets that our many populations believe. Most importantly, I accepted the premise that we need to work in unison with the elements of our climate, our planet and work with it, not against it, to achieve a more stable and desirable place to live. My early years on the farm planted a seed for me and taught me how to best tend it. I hope you, as a reader, have enjoyed my sharing and challenged your thought and consideration of my concepts and beliefs. They have served me well; hopefully, they will do the same for you.